Five Minutes More

A Wine Book for Busy People

(A sequel to 'The Five-Minute Wine Book')

Tony Aspler

To Norm Schwenker
Cheers!
Tony Aspler

For Deborah, who shares my love of wine – and the bottles.

FIVE MINUTES MORE

A Wine Book for Busy People

(A sequel to 'The Five-Minute Wine Book')

TONY ASPLER

SELF-KNOWLEDGE COLLEGE PRESS

Published by SKC PRESS

ISBN: 978-1-988277-21-9

Self-Knowledge College Press

356 Westridge Drive, Waterloo, Ontario, Canada. N2L 5Y3

Original photo Image: Lembita Mikker (Estonia)
Cover Design: Chyserr Nesti (Philippines)
MS Editor: Frank Daley (Canada)

TONY ASPLER
For wine information visit:
https://tonyaspler.com
email: tony.aspler@gmail.com

Other Inquiries: 647-205-5059 (Frank Daley)

EM: daleyfrank0@gmail.com

Five Minutes More

A Wine Book for Busy People

(A sequel to 'The Five-Minute Wine Book')

Tony Aspler

INTRODUCTION

The premise of the original 'Five Minute Wine Book' is that each chapter would take you no longer than five minutes to read.

This sequel follows the same idea and contains articles, columns and essays on wine that I have written since 2014. I am in the process of compiling it during the COVID-19 crisis. My wife Deborah and I are in self-isolation following an aborted trip to Las Vegas in March 2020.

The blog of the Vegas trip is the very last piece in this e-volume. But here are the bald facts: One morning we awoke in our bedroom at the Mandalay Bay Hotel to a message on our telephone from the management: the hotel was closing, and we were to check out my noon.

We scrambled to get a flight back to Toronto the next night (thanks to our travel agent Sandra Pauwels) and spent fourteen days at home in quarantine. To pass the time we ordered a 1000-piece jigsaw puzzle from Amazon (a sentimental painting by Norman Rockwell. It depicted the consternation caused by a small dog in a narrow alley who refused to get out of the way of a very large pizza delivery truck). If matters turned desperate, I thought, we could always eat it.

With so much time on my hands, I decided to take an inventory of my wine cellar. I found a lot of wine that should be consumed before it goes over the hill - or I do.

Being housebound, my wife and I found that we were consuming more wine than we usually do. In the past, we returned the empties to the Beer Store and received the 20-cent refund per bottle. But because of the pandemic, the Beer Store quite rightly has stopped offering that service. The net effect of this is that the empty bottles are accumulating in the garage at an alarming rate.

Which isn't altogether a bad thing, because, *in extremis*, we could soak off the labels to augment our supply of toilet paper. If, however, the lock-down goes on much longer I'll be able to see my grandchildren through university on those bottle-return deposits.

Re-reading and editing articles I have written over the past six years has been a bitter-sweet experience. Or rather an exercise in masochistic nostalgia. They reminded me how much pleasure I have experienced from the act of writing about wine – not only the remembrance of specific wines past (the Proustian madeleine dipped in tea or perhaps, more aptly, a biscotti dunked in Vin Santo), but the sheer organoleptic and intellectual enjoyment I have received from the pursuit of the fermented grape.

And it got me thinking about 55 years of writing about wine and the friendships I have made with winemakers and wine enthusiasts in Canada and around the world who share my consuming passion.

With the demise of many specialist wine magazines, the opportunity to find a home for articles like these is rapidly diminishing; and I suspect that this may well be the last of the 'Five Minute Wine Book' series.

As I turn eighty-two next year, it may be time to put away the corkscrew – in the metaphorical sense since there are wines in my cellar that need to be consumed. And when this plague has passed, I look forward to sharing them with friends and family.

In the meantime, I raise the glass at my elbow, and I wish you health. And may the Bluebird of Happiness alight on your navel and lay golden eggs.

ON OENO-PORN

Recently, my wife Deborah went to an estate sale. She returned home with a framed color photograph of what must have been an oil painting.

Its subject - two dusty bottles, Château Haut Brion 1919 and Bouchard Ainé & Fils Meursault 1904.

To the left of the bottles were a rather bedraggled label of Mas de Daumas Gassac and two corks, one branded Rausan Ségla, the other an unidentifiable St. Emilion.

To the right, a label of Château Margaux 1949, in excellent condition, and an old-fashioned corkscrew standing upright.

Now, this montage can only be described as 'oeno-porn.'

There is no other pursuit – or maybe I should say 'obsession' – that triggers the compulsion to become a collector than wine.
I'm not talking necessarily about the amassing of bottles of wine without drinking them, rather than all the appurtenances and paraphernalia that go along with the service and consumption of wine.

For the purposes of this column, I made an inventory of all the stuff we have in our house that is wine-related.

There is a cabinet full of glasses of different shapes and sizes - 150 of them, plus boxes of unused glasses in the basement (we tend to break them, so we buy them compulsively). Sitting on the top of the 500-bottle wine cabinet are 8 decanters and 2 ice buckets. In the kitchen drawer there 14 corkscrews (one of which if for left-handers) and there are others secreted around the house and in the car in case of emergency.

In the drawer where we keep the wine coasters there are 3 packets of drip stops, 8 table napkins with grape variety names and a matching tablecloth, a Coravin, and a wine aerator/strainer/pourer with stopper. In addition, there are the following: a water jug that looks like a bunch of grapes, two sets of six place mats – one featuring Bordeaux labels, the other that says *'I Sapori d'Italia,'* decorated with a bottle, glasses and grapes. There are 20-odd wine region maps, rolled up in the garage that I never look at and old wine dinner menus signed by chefs. We even have a set of place mats made from cork that we bought at MOMA in New York.

And my wife has a handbag I purchased for her in France. It's also made of cork and it can accommodate a chilled bottle and a corkscrew and that's about all.

On the wall in our kitchen is a large red and blue metal oval plaque - a genuine license to sell beverage alcohol in a Paris bistro (liberated by my French brother-in-law, no questions asked).

I also have a collection of the metal tops from champagne corks. These are called *'muselets'* (from the French verb *museler,* to muzzle.) Which make me a practicing placomusophiliac (the term for nutty collectors of these colorful discs like me). Currently, I have dozens of them sitting in a drawer, waiting to be framed.

I used to collect wine books and at one time I had over seven hundred. Now I'm down to a more reasonable one hundred. I also collect memorable bottles (empty) that have been signed by the winemaker and these have moved with me three times – much to my wife's chagrin. (Are you nodding your head now, empathizing with me or in sympathy for her?)

I also, may heaven forgive me, own a hand corking machine which I use to recork unfinished wine once I've applied the wine-preserving gas.

And don't get me started about wine labels. I use to have photo albums full of them but I donated them to my friend Alain Laliberté who is in the Guinness Book of Records as the proud owner of the world's largest collection – 230,000 and counting.

Now back to that object from the estate sale my wife brought home. It cost her $5.

I wouldn't part with it for ten times that. (Well, maybe.)

MY LIFE AS A SOMMELIER

I was a sommelier - for one night - and never again.

Torontonians who dined out in the 1980s may recall a restaurant on Carleton Street called Parkes. It was owned by my friend David Rowlands, now long-gone from the hospitality industry.

At the time I was writing the wine column for the *Toronto Star* and I thought it would make an interesting column – finding out what diners drank with their meals and how much they knew about wine.

When I asked Parkes' chef what to expect on that Saturday night, he said, gloomily, "Shrimp cocktail, steak medium-rare, ice cream, a bottle of house wine and a $2 tip."

Well, I was going to change all that and get the patrons to trade up to a good red Burgundy or a Classed Growth red Bordeaux. Rowlands knew his wines and his list reflected his taste. (We were both members of a dinner club called The Saintsbury Society, named after George Saintsbury, a Professor of French at Oxford in the 1920s who wrote a seminal wine book, entitled *Notes on A Cellar Book*. We would meet in each other's homes and the host would cook.)

Four hours of my waxing lyrical about the wines in Parkes' cellar had little effect on the clientele. But I did succeed in selling more house wine than on previous Saturday nights, a record I put down to pity.

That was then. Now Toronto diners are very sophisticated in their appreciation of wine. And gone are the days when the sommelier was a formidable apparition in a black jacket and apron with a silver tastevin around his neck – a man who would hover over you and smirk at your wine choice. Sommeliers today are young and passionate about their calling. They have taken exacting and expensive courses in the service of all beverage alcohol, buying practices, cellar management, inventory control and sales psychology.

The PhD for wine servers is to become a member of the Court of Master Sommeliers. There are 103 professionals in North America who have passed the exams and can call themselves Master Sommelier and use the honorific MS after their name. Three of them are Canadian and all live and work in Toronto – John Szabo, Jennifer Huether and Bruce Wallner. Five Canadians are currently about to take their final exam. Bruce Wallner, incidentally, just won the Best Ontario Sommelier Competition in May, beating out 15 other local wine experts. He will go on to represent Ontario in the national competition in Halifax in September.

And just what does it take to become a Master Sommelier? According to Bruce Wallner, "The cost is astronomical; the time commitment is completely not feasible for anyone wanting to have a balanced life. If I had to put a cost to it, I would say it would run to $250,000 and your commitment in terms of time would be about ten years." And where did all that money go? "Travelling and buying books, course fees, buying wine. You buy so much wine and throw it away it's disgraceful. You have to find a friend who likes to drink left-over wine, otherwise it's going to break your heart."

For two months before his final blind tasting exam Wallner sampled six wines every day at the exact time when he would be sitting the exam – 'to build up your endurance. So, every day it's six new bottles you're throwing away.'

There are four steps to the MS degree. First you must have had three years of wine service before you can take the two-day introductory course and the exam. Level II is the Certified Sommelier exam. Level III is the Advanced Sommelier Course followed by an exam and Level IV is the Master Sommelier Diploma exam. Total fees for completing all four levels are $2,745 US.

There are three parts to the Master Sommelier exam – blind tasting, theory (a panel of three Master Sommeliers fire questions at the candidate), and finally the service portion, at which there are three or four tables and the candidate has to show his or her skill at decanting, opening and serving champagne and matching food and a wine. In addition to wine management, aspirants must be on first name terms with cocktails, beers and spirits. "Basically, you come in and run a restaurant floor," says Wallner, "and they observe you and see how you do things."

A far cry from me peddling house wine in the 1980s.

THE RED IMPERATIVE

It was the French novelist and poet Henri Murger (1822-1861) who penned the injunction: 'The first duty of wine is to be red.'

He went on to say, dismissively, "Don't talk to me of your white wines."

That initial phrase has been wrongly attributed to Harry Waugh, the British wine merchant, author and a former director of Château Latour, who died in 2001 at the age of ninety-seven. Waugh added a personal preference to it by saying, 'The first duty of wine is to be red. The second is to be a Burgundy.'

And it is worth repeating here another of Harry Waugh's bon-mots. He was once asked if he had ever mistaken a claret for a Burgundy. His response: 'Not since lunch.'

This notion of red wine's supremacy is subscribed to by all civilized nations, like the Italians, the French and the Spanish. And most level-headed wine writers. So, Dionysus protect me, please, from the current fad for Raw, Natural and Orange wines or whatever you want to call them. I do not want to imbibe a white wine that tastes like a cocktail made of sherry and cider.

In the game of golf, I'm told, it is customary to shout an admonitory "Fore!" when you strike an errant ball that threatens to crown a player on the green ahead of you. The same warning should be uttered in stentorian tones when an in-coming sommelier approaches your restaurant table with the intent of palming you off with an orange wine. Because the current trend for these over-hyped wines is driven by sommeliers in search of novelty.

For those of you who have been fortunate enough not to have tasted one, an orange wine is made by fermenting white grapes on their skins for a lengthy time, giving the resulting liquid an amber or orange hue.

This caveman school of natural winemaking, without recourse to sulphur, is a throwback to how wines were originally made — usually in large terracotta amphorae known *as kvevri.* These vessels were filled with bunches of grapes, sealed and buried in the ground, sometimes for years. This was the practice in Georgia dating back to 6000 years BC. (For more information on how wine was made in this way, see **en.wikipedia.org/wiki/Kvevri**).

Well, in our enlightened times, surgeons do not operate without anesthetics; we brush our teeth to protect them; we clothe ourselves to keep warm. So why on earth would one allow wine to make itself without the discipline of a touch of sulphur and the gentle intervention of winemaker as midwife?

To forego the use of sulphur in the winemaking process is akin to walking around with body odor. A soupçon of sulphur protects the wine against oxidation, stabilizes its color and gives it shelf-life.

Don't be deterred by the ominous warning on the back label of all wines that proclaims the bottle "Contains Sulphites." All wines — and anything that undergoes fermentation, like cheese and sauerkraut — will contain Sulphites; some sulphite is created naturally by the transformative act of fermentation.

So, to be accurate, that cautionary phrase should read "Guaranteed to contain Sulphites."

And what's next in the never-ending quest for the new thing in the world of wine? Since we already have red wine, white wine, pink wine, black wine (from Cahors) and green wine (Vinho Verde from Portugal — though it isn't actually green, except maybe with the addition of a little food-grade green dye on St Patrick's Day) — how about blue wine to complete the rainbow?

End of rant. But I predict this orange wine fad will not endure and I for one will not mourn its passing. After all, the first duty of wine is to be drinkable.

WHATEVER'S ON THE TABLE

Maybe I'm getting impatient or maybe I'm just too bored with wading through all the literature on the intricacies of matching food and wine — a minor portion of which, I confess, I have contributed over the years in several books and many articles. But I no longer give a damn about the wine's color as long as there is a bottle of it on the table at dinner.

I have given up fussing over which wine will go best with boeuf bourguignonne (even if the answer is in the name) or with Caesar salad (Sauvignon Blanc) or with gravad lax (iced vodka is amazing).

I have decided to take a leaf out of the Italian songbook and drink red with everything. Well, almost everything. I recall a visit to Château de Fargues in Sauternes a few years ago where they served their sweet wine at lunch with oysters! (Not as heretical as you might think.) And even further back, in the early 1980s when I was a neophyte wine writer still wet behind the palate, I visited Serego Alghero in Veneto. My host, Count Pieralvise di Serego Alighieri poured a glass of his Amarone in his living room and then passed around a bowl of After Eight chocolate mints.

I thought it was a test and that if I knew anything about wine, I was meant to refuse it. But he insisted. And yes, his 15.5% alcohol Amarone went shoulder to shoulder with the chocolate mint with no ill effects to either party.

But back to my nightly dining preferences. It's not that I don't like white wine but — with apologies to Montrachet and Pouilly-Fumé — I have always thought of white wine as foreplay and red as the main event. Maybe I'm addicted to tannin.

For the past forty years or so, the license plate on my car has been CLARET — what the British call red Bordeaux, a wine I was brought up on in England when I first discovered the glories of the fermented grape. But sadly, I have had to retire it as I have just bought a hybrid car and you can't, it seems, get a vanity plate in green yet.

The Italians, although they produce some great white wines from Friuli to Sicily, are basically red wine drinkers, as I mentioned — even serving it with grilled fish. In 1989, my American wine writer colleagues, David Rosengarten and Joshua Wesson — who sound like a law firm — co-authored a book that challenged our preconceived notions about wine prohibitions.

The title said it all: *Red Wine with Fish*.

Rosengarten and Wesson argued that it wasn't the color of the wine that mattered when it came to matching with fish but the amount of acidity in the wine — that cool climate red wines like Burgundy and Valpolicella had enough acidity to cut through the oiliness of fish, especially when served chilled to accentuate the perception of the acid.

In the final analysis there is one wine that goes perfectly with everything, from soup to nuts or just by itself; if I were to win the lottery, I would stock it by the case. And that is Champagne: Blanc de Blancs, Blanc de Noirs and blends. Preferably in magnums.

The final word on the subject I leave to the British thriller writer, Gavin Lyall, who had this advice on serving wine in a bed-sitter: 'Always match the drinks to the color of the carpet.'

A QUESTION OF TASTE

The most frequently asked question of a wine writer is, 'What's a good wine under $10?' And this is usually followed up by, 'What's *your* favorite wine?'

While I'm prepared to answer the first question with a little thought, I have no hesitation in responding to the second. Within a heartbeat I will tell you that it was a bottle of Domaine Comte Georges de Vogüé Musigny Cuvée Vieilles Vignes 1964 - a magnificent Grand Cru red Burgundy - and I drank it on February 13th, 1975. That was the day my son Guy was born. It was fantastic but then I was ready to receive a great bottle of wine. I drank it alone that evening as Guy's mother was otherwise occupied.

I am convinced that the pleasure you derive from a bottle of wine has very little to do with its quality or price and everything to do with your mood, the company and the ambiance. Imagine for a moment that you are invited to dinner by your bank manager. (OK, pause for suspension of disbelief.) He has opened a bottle of Château Latour 1961, a First Growth claret from an exceptional year. (OK, so this really is fantasy.) But just as you are about to raise the glass to you lips, he says, 'The reason I invited you here this evening is that, unfortunately, I have to tell you that I'm foreclosing on your mortgage.'

That once-in-a-lifetime wine, coveted by all collectors, is going to taste like ashes in your mouth.

On the other hand, picture yourself at a picnic with someone you love. The sun is shining; the birds are singing; the ants are at bay. You have a round of Camembert, some pâté, a French baguette and cooling in the stream is a simple bottle of Beaujolais that you and your loved one are about to imbibe from paper cups. That wine, I guarantee, will taste like the nectar of the gods.

Here's another anecdote to underline the point. My first visit to Bordeaux was in 1966. One of my appointments was at Château Palmer in the Margaux commune. I was shown around by the late Peter A. Sichel (not to be confused with his cousin Peter M. F. Sichel, whose company created the German Riesling, Blue Nun.

Peter A. toured me around the picture-book building with its grey slate roof and four pointed towers. Then he took me upstairs to the second floor where there were rooms that looked like dormitories, equipped with rows of iron bedsteads. On the walls was graffiti written in German. Peter explained to me that Château Palmer had been occupied by German troops during the Second World War. Châteaux Lafite-Rothschild and Mouton-Rothschild in Pauillac, he told me, were not garrisoned with German troops, because these were Jewish properties which had been appropriated by the Third Reich.

After that morning visit, I went to lunch at a restaurant in St. Emilion on a hill overlooking the town. It was a brilliant sunny day and our party opted to eat outside. We ordered the house wine which was delicious – so much so that I ordered two bottles to take home to London with me.
In the following February, on a grey, wet, miserable day that you can only experience in an English winter, I opened one of the bottles to try to recapture the memory of that lunch and the visit to Palmer. The wine was awful. I had to pour it down the sink.

Wine is liquid memory, at least for me. I recall events by the wine I was drinking at the time. I can tell you the wine that I shared with my first wife the night I proposed to her (or did she propose to me?).

It was a Château Haut-Brion 1954, not a great year. I can remember the vintage of the wine and what it tasted like but I can't recall the date or year of that engagement dinner. I am in good company in this regard when I recall a quote uttered over one hundred years ago, by the Anglo-French writer Hilaire Belloc. In an address to the Saintsbury Club at Vintners' Hall in London he declaimed: 'When that this too, too solid flesh shall melt, and I am called before my Heavenly Father, I shall say to him Sir, I don't remember the name of the village, and I don't remember the name of the girl, but the wine was Chambertin.'

A great Pinot Noir, like the Comte de Vogüé Musigny '64, can do that to you. (The Saintsbury Club, incidentally, was named for George Saintsbury, the English literary critic who wrote 'Notes of a Cellar Book,' arguably the first book about how to appreciate wine.)

On the subject of my son's birth date wine, I checked on the Internet for what I would have to pay today for a bottle of Comte de Vogüé Musigny Cuvée Vieilles Vignes 1964. Bottles have been sold in the Netherland and Germany the price of which averaged at around $3,000 a bottle. But to me the memory of that evening and the reason for it were priceless.

MYSTICAL ORGANIC: BIODYNAMIC VINEYARDS

One of the last series of lectures that the Austrian philosopher Rudolph Steiner gave in 1924 was to a group of German farmers. They were worried about the effects on their land, livestock and crops resulting from the use of chemical fertilizers, herbicides and pesticides.

Those eight lectures Steiner delivered at a conference in Koberwitz, a year before his death, formed the basis of what we know today as the biodynamic movement. His thesis was that farmers must return to pre-industrial methods to grow their crops and tend their soil. A return to peasant farming, as it were. Farmers, advised Steiner, should adjust their activities to the rhythms of Nature and become aware of the cycles of the moon and planets and their link to the health of all living things on earth.

'In Nature,' he wrote, 'and actually throughout the universe, everything is in mutual interaction with everything else. In this materialistic age of ours, we follow up only on the coarser kinds of interplay...'

The aim of biodynamics, as Steiner expressed it, is to create a healthy soil ecosystem by choosing to use natural compost over chemical products and to plant and harvest by the phases of the moon. Organic farming just shuns chemical products while biodynamic growing takes a more holistic approach, treating the soil itself as a living organism.

No sector has embraced Steiner's vision more enthusiastically than the wine industry.

By 2011 (the latest figures available) some 642,000 acres of wines worldwide were cultivated according to organic farming regulations. While this is a mere 4 per cent of global grape-growing, the increase in organically-managed vineyards since 2004 has been three-fold, which suggest even more growth in the future.

The largest vineyard surfaces farmed organically are in Spain, France and Italy. Soon China will join the list.

It is Steiner's concept of composting that makes non-believers roll their eyes. He devised plant-based sprays against infections that are made up of composted material found around the farm. The compost is diluted with water to make a kind of herbal tea.

But here's where we enter the realm of voodoo science: the compost's effectiveness is enhanced by the addition of fresh cow manure that has been packed into a cow's horn and buried in the vineyard at the fall equinox and dug up in the spring. The fermented material from the cow's horn is then mixed with water and sprayed over the vineyard. The recipe is one hornful per hectare (2.47 acres).

Steiner explained it this way: '...by burying the cow horn with the manure in it, we preserve in the horn the etheric and astral forces that the horn was accustomed to reflect when it was on the cow. Because the cow horn is now outwardly surrounded by the Earth, all the Earth's etherizing and astralizing rays stream into its inner cavity.' The result is the fermented manure is transformed into 'an extremely concentrated, enlivening and fertilizing force.'

Cue the eye rolling.

The question is, of course, does biodynamics work? Does it make for a more balanced vineyard and for wines that taste better than those that have been produced using chemical products?

In February of this year I attended Millésime Bio in Montpellier, France. In three hangar-sized halls, 800 biodynamic and organic wineries were showing their products. One of the wineries was Domaine Cazes of Rivesaltes in the Languedoc-Roussillon. The proprietor, Emanuel Cazes, toured me around his vineyard and showed me the constituents of the 'tea' he sprays over his vineyard soil – nettles, horsetail and willow leaves which he steeped in boiling water and mixed with the cow dung.

Other producers, he told me, use yarrow, chamomile, oak bark, dandelion and valerian - all of which were prescribed by Rudolph Steiner. Cazes says that after fifteen years of practicing biodynamic farming the pH of his wines is lower (pH is the measure of the degree of relative acidity as opposed to the relative alkalinity of any liquid. It's measured from 0 to 14, with 7 being neutral and 2 being lemon juice. Wines with a low pH - between 3 and 3.4 - will taste tart and crisp). And as a result of the application of the sprays, the roots of Cazes' vines, he says, are deeper which means he is able to extract more trace minerals from the soil, making for more complex flavors in his wines.

Certainly, the concept of biodynamics is in sync with our contemporary concern with the environment as well as the romantic notion of a return to a simpler way of farming. But if you put two glasses of wine in front of me – one made without recourse to sulphur products, and one made the 'traditional' way – I don't think I could tell the difference. Yet for all its hocus-pocus I would like to think that biodynamic winemaking works. And for producers who want to convert their vineyards to biodynamic, it takes three years to get certification, as long as the wind doesn't carry chemical sprays from your neighbor's farm. From then on, it's a leap of faith.

PINNING THE BUTTERFLY

Delving serendipitously into my favourite reference book, *Brewer's Dictionary of Phrase and Fable*, I came across the term, 'Gleipnir.'

Definition: In Scandinavian legend, the chain by which the wolf Fenrir was bound. It was extremely light and made from the noise made by the footfalls of a cat, the roots of mountains, the sinews of bears, the breath of fishes, the beards of women and the spittle of birds.

Which got me thinking about the flights of fancy some of my wine-writing brethren are prone to when it comes to describing the aromas and tastes of wine.

I have been guilty of adjectival excesses myself, having once described an Alsace Gewürztraminer as 'a lumberjack wearing too much after-shave.' But now I realize it was a mere conceit and not something that helps a prospective consumer make a purchasing decision.

A small quiz here. To what or to whom do the following two quotations refer: 'Raspberry scented like the breezes from the Islands of the Blessed, a dream of grace and delicacy, the twinkling feet of dancing nymphs suddenly set free in our tedious world ...'

'They opened the gates of Paradise which Swinburne fathered on Swedenborg where all the senses were confounded and where music, color and perfume were one.'

Believe it or not, both refer to bottles of wine. Not just any wine. These panegyrics were penned by two British connoisseurs in the 1940s. They allude, respectively, to a tasting of Château Margaux 1871 and Château La Lagune 1858 — wines made during the Golden Age of Claret before the dreaded Phylloxera blight laid waste the vineyards of Europe. They say that Bordeaux reds have never been quite as good since. But then, they always say that about all Golden Ages.

I surfed the net looking for some contemporary examples of purple prose in wine writing and found this award-winner: 'Dark and packed with a large core of hoisin sauce, Port reduction, bittersweet cocoa, raw steak, raspberry ganache and charcoal that manages to stay fleshy and driven through the long, structured finish. A stallion of a wine. Offers youthful impact now, but really built for cellaring — unlike most of its peers, which offer vivid fruit right out of the gate.' (The wine in question was a $44 Chilean red.)

Other runners-up were: 'Essence of the felt in the case of a Stradivarius violin case' and, 'Reminds me of the sharp keys on a well-tuned Steinway — only the sharp keys!'

The best wine writing should make you salivate and should convey the taster's enthusiasm for the product. Any analogies should be democratically universal and comprehensible (not: 'Smells like my grandmother's knitting box'). Above all, it should avoid references to medical conditions, body parts or the writer's matrimonial problems. And shun such weasel words as 'interesting' and 'complex.' They sound like the answers to survey questions about a first date.

And then there's the minimalist school of wine writing, as advocated by my old friend Tim Hanni, America's first Master of Wine, a trained chef and the man who entered the term "umami" into the wine lexicon. For I have quoted him elsewhere in this book for his one-word descriptors, either thumbs up or thumbs down: either 'Yum' or 'Yuck.'

Harking back to my opening sentence, Mr. Brewer also enlightened me as to the derivation of the word 'serendipity'. Apparently, it was coined by Horace Walpole, the eighteenth-century historian, politician and novelist. Walpole formed it based on the title of a fairy story, *The Three Princes of Serendip*, because the princes "were always making discoveries, by accidents and sagacity, of things they were not in quest of.'"

Bless you, the Reverend Ebenezer Cobham Brewer for your erudition and the volume you gave the world in 1870. It should be on every wine writer's shelf.

REFLECTIONS ON A BUSMAN'S HOLIDAY: A TUSCAN VILLA AND A VERONESE APARTMENT

If the health inspectors of Verona will permit, I would like my ashes scattered on the floor of the Antica Bottega del Vino - the best wine bar in the world. Forget Juliet's balcony with all its lovelorn graffiti and head to this gem tucked away on a tiny alley called Via Scudo di Francia just off the Piazza del Erbe. It's a place of pilgrimage for the true lover of wine.

Established in 1890, the Bottega's wine collection is one of the best in Italy with 18,000 bottles in the rabbit warren of cellars that nestle into a Roman wall. The Bottega's list is 165 pages of the finest producers from Italy and around the world. There is a huge chest of drawers down there filled with vintages of Quintarelli Amarones and Domaine de la Romanée-Conti. You want Château Pétrus, Grange, Krug and Yquem? It's all there; but the pride of the collection are the wines from the Italian provinces and particularly the range of local Amarones.

When I first visited the Bottega in the mid-1980s the owner would stand at the bar and announce winemakers when they entered as if they were visiting movie stars: 'Angelo Gaja!... Giorgio Grai!...Giacomo Bologna!' And we would repair down to the cellar and pull bottles from the racks to have with steaming plates of pasta. Those days are gone but the kitchen is still great, the snacks at the bar are still delicious and the selection of wines by the glass is enormous.

****

The first Italian wine I ever purchased was in London in 1966. It was the Masi Campofiorin 1964, the original vintage of a wine that would introduce the world to the concept of *ripasso*. This time-honored process was used by the peasant farmers of Veneto to add body and structure to their Valpolicella. The newly-made wine was re-fermented on the lees (the dead yeast cells, grapes skins and seeds) of their Amarone production.

The grapes for Amarone are dried for up to 120 days on racks before they are fermented to concentrate their sugars. Sandro Boscaini, the owner of Masi, a.k.a. Mr. Amarone, refined and modernized the technique by adding partially dried grapes to his young Valpolicella. He registered the name Ripasso to refer to this method but ultimately donated the trademark to the Verona Chamber of Commerce. Now virtually all the 70-plus Amarone producers in the region make a Ripasso wine. Masi produces five different Amarones and was the first producer to make single vineyard Amarones, each with a recognizable terroir character.

****

If a noble Tuscan family like the Frescobaldis can survive for thirty-two generations, there are bound to be some black sheep lurking under the family free. And being a wine family, their exploits might just be memorialized in wine. Frescobaldi's Quaranta Altari ('Forty Churches') Vin Santo recalls the penance of an early eighteenth-century ancestor named Bartolomeo Frescobaldi. This sociable Marquese held a Ballo Angelico – a pagan rite where the participants danced naked - at his Villa di Montecastello in Tuscany.

Gossip about the party reached Rome and Bartolomeo was summarily excommunicated by Pope Clement XI. Determined to get back into the Church, the chastened Bartolomeo made the journey to Rome on foot to beg forgiveness. The Pope finally exonerated him when he promised to build forty churches around the Val de Pesa area in the Province of Florence. Interesting that the commemorative wine should a Vin Santo – Italy's 'holy wine.'

The contemporary Marquesi de' Frescobaldi have another fascinating connection with miscreants. Between Corsica and Livorno is a small island called Gorgona which could be called Italy's Alcatraz. The monastery on the island that dates back to the Middle Ages was appropriated in 1869 and turned into what is euphemistically called today an 'agricultural penal colony.'

The inmates make cheese, and, under the supervision of Frescobaldi winemakers, a wine called Gorgona, a blend of Ansonica and Vermentino grapes. The first vintage of Gorgona was 2012 and proceeds from the sale of the small production support the rehabilitation efforts for members of the colony.

****

If you're talking about Castello di Volpaia in Tuscany, you might say it takes a hamlet to raise a winery. You wouldn't know that wine was produced here because the fermenting and ageing cellars, the barrel rooms and bottling plant are hidden inside churches, houses and in subterranean passages all connected by pipes under the cobbled streets. The same goes for the press house for Castello di Volpaia olive oil. This 12th century fortified village, set on one of the highest hills in Tuscany, looks like a sleepy place well off the usual tourist route. But Giovanella Stenti and her family who own the village, literally lock, stock and barrel, run a thriving business, employing directly or indirectly the 60-odd inhabitants of Volpaia. They also run a wine bar and an open-air restaurant.

****

And that, gentle reader, is how I spent my summer holidays.

Ciao.

VERMENTINO, MY VALENTINE

If I'm allowed a say in these things, my vote for the Next Big Thing is Vermentino. This light-skinned grape, masquerading under 40 different synonyms, is planted mainly in Corsica, Sardinia, Tuscany and Liguria (where it's known as Pigato) and Piemonte (as Favorita). There are also plantings in the Languedoc and Roussillon (where it's known as Rolle); but its finest expression comes from Sardinia where it represents the most widely planted variety, red or white.

In other words, Vermentino is a grape that likes warm, dry weather which is why it can be found in the following Californian wineries' portfolios: Tablas Creek in Paso Robles, Mahoney Vineyards in the Napa Carneros, Uvaggio Vineyards in Lodi, and Thornton Winery in Temecula. And over eighty wineries in Australia from McLaren Vale to Margaret River grow this varietal.

So why haven't we heard more about this interesting wine in Ontario rather than being subjected to the oceans of Chardonnay and Pinot Grigio that flood the shelves? At the time of writing, Quebec's SAQ lists sixteen Vermentino offerings and BC's LDB three and Ontario's LCBO, one.

I first tasted Vermentino eleven years ago over lunch in the Cantinetta Antinori in Florence (the restaurant on the ground floor of the Antinori palazzo - a 'must stop' for anyone visiting that amazing city). The wine was a revelation – crisp and delicate with a light aromatic note and flavors of white peach and citrus fruit with a thread of minerality. I asked my host Piero Antinori about it and he told me the grapes came from the family's Guado al Tasso estate in Bolgheri on the Tuscan coast; but only a small quantity was produced which is why we didn't see it in our market.

In the following years I have sought out Vermentino on wine lists wherever I've dined and happily it is beginning to show up more often. And last December I visited Sardinia, the spiritual home of the grape.

DNA analysis suggests that Vermentino might be related to the Hungarian Furmint, the principal grape used in the production of the dessert wine, Tokaji; and certainly, the dry version of Furmint is quite similar in style to Vermentino. There is some question, however, as to whether the variety was imported into Italy from Hungary or whether the grape migrated from Italy to Hungary. Whatever its provenance, it has become the signature wine of Sardinia.

On Italy’s second largest island, after Sicily, Vermentino is grown in the northern province of Olbia-Tempio in an area known as the Gallura region. There is documentation placing the earliest reference to Vermentino being cultivated here that goes back to the fourteenth century. These vineyards are usually planted on slopes facing the sea so that the reflected light assists the ripening process.

Although the salt sea air does impart a discreet salinity to the flavor of the wine (rather like the coastal Manzanilla sherries of Sanlucar de Barrameda.) While the Gallura denomination – a DOCG – is considered the best expression of this grape, Vermentino is also grown in the south of the island where it is produced mainly as either a sweet wine, a blended wine or a sparkler.

Producers of Sardinian Vermentino to look for are Costamolino from Argiolas, Funtanaliras from the Cantina del Vermentino Monti, Cantine di Gallura, Surrau Branu Vermentino di Gallura and Sella & Mosca La Cala. And in its sparkling version - Piero Mancini Vermentino di Gallura Spumante Brut. From other Italian regions, look for Castello di Volpaia Prelius Vermentino from Maremma, Banfi La Pettegola Vermentino from Bolgheri and from Antinori's estate Le Mortelle, in Castiglione della Pescaia, a wine called Le Mortelle Vivia, a blend of Vermentino, Viognier and Ansonica - one of the most exciting Italian whites I have tasted.

FIFTY SHADES OF PINK

Back in the day, real men didn't eat quiche. And we would rather be seen wearing an apron at the kitchen sink than be caught holding a glass of rosé. Pink wines were for girls. For men, these pretty wines were neither fish, nor fowl, nor good red herring.

How times have changed. A research study by VinExpo on international wine trends found that the consumption of rosé wines in Canada shot up 38% between 2007 and 2012. And this wasn't just women drinking them. The Vinexpo study forecasts even greater growth of 45.5% between 2014 and 2016. Admittedly this is from a small base, but these growth numbers are impressive.

'There was a time when you would never see a man caught dead drinking a glass of rosé,' says Shari Mogk-Edwards, the then Vice President of Marketing at the LCBO. 'It's totally different now.'

I can't figure out the sudden allure for these cheerleaders of the wine world, other than ascribing it to the Carousel Effect – what goes around, comes around. I'd bet a dollar to a donut that your very first taste of wine was a sparkling rosé. How can you forget Mateus Rosé? It was like your first kiss.

There are some wine regions that take rosé seriously – Tavel, across the Rhône River from Châteauneuf-du-Pape, and Bandol, east of Marseille, for example, and the commune of Marsannay in Burgundy – but for the most part rosé is a by-product of red wine-making. And it's an ideal wine for cool climate regions, like Ontario, where black grapes don't necessarily ripen every year.

Apart from a few *teinturier* varieties that yield deeply colored juice, most wine grapes deliver clear, white juice. If this juice is fermented without contact with the skins it will produce a white wine. You may have seen champagne labelled *Blanc de Noirs* which means a white wine made from Pinot Noir and Pinot Meunier – both black grapes.

To make red wine winemakers must macerate the skins of black grapes with the juice.

The acid in the juice breaks down the cells in the skins and releases color. (It also releases tannins and resveratrol but that's another story.) If winemakers leave the skins in contact with the fermenting juice for 12 to 24 hours, depending on the variety, they will make a pink wine; a week or two weeks' contact will produce a deeply colored red wine.

But in cool climate regions winemakers may want to intensify the color of their red wines by bleeding off liquid during the fermentation process to create a higher ratio of skins to juice. What they bleed off will be rosé wine. This technique is known as *saignée,* from the French term, bleeding (which sounds more tasteful than its French synonym, *phlébotomie*).

There are three ways to make rosé - skin contact for a short time, bleeding off juice from vats during traditional fermentation, or by blending red wine with white to reach the desired shade of pink. An example of this latter method (frowned upon in Europe) is Henry of Pelham's Pink House Wine Company Chardonnay Merlot 2012. As its label tells you in all honesty, the wine is a blend of Chardonnay and Merlot.

This method is outlawed in France but – and there is always a 'but' in French wine law - the practice of cutting white wine with red is permitted for the production of rosé champagne. Although some champagne houses still use the *saignée* process, most of them now blend red and white wines because it's much easier that way to reach a consistent pink color from vintage to vintage.

There is a huge range of colors for rosé wines from the palest onion skin and a grey-pink shade the French call *l'oeil-de-perdrix* (eye of the partridge) to different hues of salmon, amber and orange to pale, light and deep ruby. There is no regulation that governs what color a rosé should be, merely a descriptor after the fact. The *Conseil Interprofessionnel des Vins de Provence* has made a brave stab at producing a scale. The bureaucrats have determined the six main colors of rosé wines made in their region. Each color refers to a fruit: Gooseberry, Peach, Grapefruit, Cantaloupe, Mango and Mandarin (see **http://www.vinsdeprovence.com/en/focus-on-rose/publication-and-works**).

With the range of colors goes a range of tastes and styles. The black grape used will determine part of the taste profile, but its ultimate flavor will rest on the amount of residual sugar left in the wine. European rosés are generally drier than New World rosés with Blush wines being the sweetest.

Blush entered the wine lexicon in 1972 when Sutter Hill winemaker Bob Trinchero had a problem with his California Zinfandel. The fermentation stuck, leaving the wine a pale color with a high percentage of unfermented sugar. Since rosé was a moribund category, Trinchero marketed his mistake as a 'blush wine' called White Zinfandel. Sales in 1980 were 25,000 cases. Four years later Sutter Home White Zin soared to 1.5 million cases.

So, rosés of all hues are here to stay, it seems. Join the trend: drink pink and make the boys wink.

THE EAST IS RED AND MAYBE WHITE AS WELL

I'm going to stick my neck out and make a bold prediction. Please tear this column out and seal it in an envelope, put it in a safe place and don't open it until 2054.

I predict that within two generations China will produce wines that will rival the best that Bordeaux and Burgundy have to offer.

The first time I tasted Chinese wine was at a banquet in 1978 in Toronto's late lamented Sai Woo restaurant. I couldn't drink them. Ten years later I was in China to visit the first Sino-French Joint Venture Winery, a co-production between the Chinese government and Rémy Martin. The wines were marketed under the Dynasty label and they've appeared from time to time on liquor board shelves here. The Dynasty wines were an improvement but not something I would actually shell out money for.

So, what do I base the declaration that China will be producing great wines by 2054? A twelve-day visit to Wuwei City located at the eastern end of the Hexi Corridor, part of the old Silk Road. The corridor in Ganzu province is a string of oases that runs along the northern edge of Tibetan Plateau leading to the Gobi Desert. In 2012 Wuwei City was named, 'The Wine City of China' by the China Food Industry Association - as being the most important of the country's nine major wine regions.

Fifteen per cent of all China's grapes come from the Hexi Corridor. This arid region receives a meagre six and a half inches of rain a year which means the grape farmers don't need to use fungicides and pesticides in their vineyards, making it the world's largest organic vineyard surface.

This desert and semi-desert wine-growing region along the Hexi Corridor is between latitudes 36° and 40°, a band that includes Bordeaux and the Napa Valley. The sandy soil here also supports the cultivation of melons, apricots, peaches, pears, cherries, wheat, potatoes, onions and, of course, corn. More corn than you can shake a cob at. Also, you see endless fields of marigolds, the petals of which are used in the manufacture of shampoos and face creams and for eye health.

The main grape varieties planted here are the cherished European vinifera - Pinot Noir, Merlot, Cabernet Franc, Cabernet Sauvignon, Chardonnay and Riesling. The Chinese consume one liter of wine a year; but we're talking about a population of 1.351 billion (a 2012figure). All they need to do to empty the world's cellars is to up their consumption by another liter. (Canada's wine consumption per capita is currently 15 liters per annum). At the 3rd Organic Wine Festival of China Hexi Corridor in August last year I witnessed how a generation of young Chinese have taken to wine. During a huge outdoor tasting the hundreds of participants hung on every word of the sommeliers and wine journalists who addressed them while they happily quaffed whatever was put down in front of them.

Wine production in China grew by 20 per cent between 2006 and 2011 and is projected to rise by 54 per cent by next year. Everything about the Chinese wine industry is monumentally big. The six enterprises based in the Hexi Corridor crushed 86,000 tons of grapes in 2012.

The Gansu Grand Dragon Organic Wine Company, the largest in the region and China's first all-organic enterprise with a staff of 4,000, is in the process of planting 66,667 hectares of vines. (All of Bordeaux measures just over 120,000 hectares; Napa has 17,637 hectares of vines). The company's massive chateau that looks like an Egyptian necropolis has a storage capacity of 100,000 tons.

The purpose of my visit to China was to consult, along with four other wine experts, on a new winery to be built in the city of Linze. The entrepreneur behind the venture is a Chinese businessman named Jason Tang who imports and bottles wines from California's Central Valley. Our group toured local vineyards to see how the local farmers grew their grapes. At a city named Bangiao we walked through a 134-acre vineyard farmed by 30 different farmers.

Eighty per cent of the vineyard was planted to Cabernet Sauvignon and Merlot augmented by some table grape varieties. The varying levels of expertise and commitment by the collective were evident row by row. The agronomist who showed us around explained that along the Hexi Corridor they have to bury their vines for winter and uncover them in April – just as the growers in Quebec and Prince Edward County have to do.

During my stay, I tasted as many locally-made wines as I could and was impressed by their authenticity; they actually tasted of the variety that appeared on the label. They're not there yet but with more care taken in the vineyard and a willingness to learn from the experience of established wine regions I'm convinced that Chinese wines will be on the tables of the best restaurants around the world in the not too distant future. And at prices that we can all afford.

WINE AND THE BIBLE

'Wine,' wrote Hippocrates, the father of Western medicine, 'is a matter which in a miraculous way (is) intended for men to apply in good and bad health in the proper quantities.'

The Greek physician was born in 460 BC. He obviously enjoyed a glass or two because he lived to the ripe old age of eighty-three at a time when the average life expectancy in Greece was thirty years.

Hippocrates' words on the health-giving benefits of wine are echoed by the Apostle Paul in his letter to Timothy: 'No longer drink only water, but use a little wine for the sake of your stomach and your frequent ailments.' (Timothy 5:23)

This theme of praising the medicinal effects of wine, rather than the sensual enjoyment of wine, dates back to ancient Egyptian papyri and Sumerian tablets inscribed over 4,000 years ago.

Both Testaments of the Bible are replete with references to wine, references that are at one and the same time literal, symbolic and metaphorical. The proliferation of these references speaks to the importance of the fermented grape in the daily lives of Israelites and the newly-converted Christians of the New Testament. From Noah planting the first vineyard after the Flood to the Wedding at Cana, when Jesus turns water into wine, the presence of wine in daily life is celebrated and, when taken to excess, deprecated.

But of all biblical references to wine, arguably the most significant occurred at the Last Supper. During this Passover meal, with wine and unleavened bread central to the ritual, Jesus posited the concept of the Eucharist. According to the Book of Matthew, after blessing the bread he broke it and gave pieces to his disciples, saying, 'This is my body.' Then he blessed the wine and instructed those present, 'Drink of it, all of you, for this is my blood of the covenant, which is poured out for many for the forgiveness of sins.'

Significantly, it was wine that Jesus chose as symbolic of his life rather than beer or mead (fermented honey), both of which predate wine. This would suggest that wine was the preferred beverage of the populace at the time (unlike today when beer is the beverage of choice and mead is virtually ignored).

As in our era, biblical references reflect an ambivalent attitude towards the consumption of wine and by extension the imbibing of any alcoholic beverage that can lead to intoxication.

This dichotomy of thinking about alcohol is still with us today. Wine is a gift of God (or, for the ancients, the gods) that can bestow pleasure and delight on a community or degradation and destruction on individuals who take it to extremes. If one needed a biblical injunction to enjoy the pleasures of the table, you need look no further than Ecclesiastes 9:7: 'Go, eat your food with gladness, and drink your wine with a joyful heart, for it is now that God favors what you do.'

The consequence of that license to imbibe could be overindulgence. The first documented instance of drunkenness in the Old Testament is poor old Noah, the original mega-boat builder and Captain turned zookeeper. According to Genesis (9:18) 'Noah was the first tiller of the soil. He planted a vineyard; and he drank of the wine, and became drunk, and lay uncovered in his tent.'

Michelangelo painted a fresco in the Sistine Chapel entitled 'Drunkenness of Noah' that depicts the inebriated patriarch being covered with a cloak by his son Ham to hide his nakedness. Noah's other two sons, Shem and Japheth, look on. Ironically, everyone in the fresco is naked except for an agricultural worker outside the tent who is nonchalantly tilling the soil fully clothed.

Obviously, biblical times there must have been a lot of people who were not aware of 'the elephant in the room,' because drunkenness, viewed as a sin, is mentioned either metaphorically or literally more than seventy times in the Bible. (There are, however, no biblical admonitions against dancing which, as we are well aware, can lead to twerking.)

Interestingly, in the Hebrew Bible there are ten different words for wine and in the Greek Bible, only five. If you apply the syllogism that the Inuit have an unusually large number of words for snow because of their familiarity with it, then the Jews must be more intimately acquainted with wine than their Christian brethren. But not only is this false logic but the premise is invalid since a linguist named Laura Martin proved that Eskaluet, a series of languages native to the Arctic Rim countries, 'have about the same number of distinct word roots referring to snow as English does...'

Suffice it to say that I am in full agreement with my fellow wine writer, Saint Paul, when it comes to the medicinal properties of wine; and I would go even further by having the words of the late André Simon tattooed across my chest - if I was of that mind. Simon, a great gourmand and founder of The International Wine & Food Society, wrote in his book, 'The Art of Great Living': 'Wine is purer than either water or milk because no typhoid or other deadly germ can live in wine.'

André Simon died in 1970 at the age of 93.

I rest my case.

YOU SAY TOMATO AND I SAY WINE

I can now strike off one destination from my bucket list. In August my wife Deborah and I toured Charlevoix's Flavour Trail in Quebec. We stayed at Hotel Le Germain Charlevoix in Baie-Saint-Paul, a spanking new complex that was awarded the world's best hotel design in 2013.

The only way I can describe its ultra-modern architecture is as 'industrial-pastoral.' It stands on the site of what used to be Quebec's biggest wooden barn that was once owned by nuns - Les Petites Franciscaines de Marie de Baie-Saint-Paul – and was destroyed by fire in 2007. A model of the original stands in the courtyard.

We had mapped out our visits to the artisanal producers along the food route that takes you north up Route 381 from Baie-Saint-Paul and to L'Isle-aux-Coudres, a twenty-minute drive east of the town. There's a free two-kilometer ferry ride to the island where we lunched at Boulangerie Bouchard (established 1945 and famous for its Tarte Grand-mère and sugar pies) before visiting **Cidrerie Vergers Pedneault** to sample their cider and fruit wines; and then on to **Les Moulins de l'Isle-aux-Coudres**, a functioning 1825 watermill and 1836 windmill where they grind flour.

Our first stop the next day was to La Ferme Basque where Isabelle Mihura and her partner Jacques Etcheberrigaray keep 4500 ducks – Mulards for foie gras and Muscovy ducks for meat. Apparently, only males are force-fed for foie gras. The females are kept for their eggs.

Next stop, Quebec's only emu farm where Raymonde Tremblay rears 400 emus for their meat; the oil from their fat she uses to manufacture skin creams and lip balms. She sells jars of her own emu cassoulet and her special emu spaghetti sauce. (Here I learned that emus grow six-foot in a year and they can't walk backwards. Who knew?)

But the most surprising find of all was 'The World's First Tomato wine.'

Yes, a wine made from tomatoes. At Domaine de la Vallée de Bras, Pascal Miche and his wife Lucie have been producing wine from fermented tomatoes for five years. They use a recipe developed by Pascal's Belgian great-grandfather in 1938. His name was Omer and the brand for their tomato wine is called Omerto in homage to him. They make four different products from three varieties of organically-grown heirloom tomatoes – Dry, Sweet, Semi-Dry aged in acacia wood, and a Sweet version aged in cherry and chestnut casks.

They have some 4,000 tomato plants in their 'vineyard' on the slopes of rang Saint-Antoine Nord and they produce on average 15,000 litres. The tomatoes are harvested in mid-August to the mid-September at 25 to 26 Brix and have to be chaptalized to get the 'wine' up to 16% alcohol. The fermentation ('our yeast is a secret') takes five months.

It's very much a hands-on operation with five people involved in the harvesting, crushing, fermenting in stainless steel tanks, filtering, bottling and labelling of the bottles. They now export their products to Hong Kong, Japan and the US.

Deborah and I tasted through the range and we were very surprised by the quality. The dry 'wine' is golden in color and tasted like sake with no suggestion of tomato flavor. The sweet version has a nose of orange blossom, honey, melon and lychee. The acacia-aged version has a malt whisky character and the chestnut/cherry-aged wine smells of rose petals and cherries and resembles an off-dry sherry. Pascal says that his wines – which are vintage-dated – can last for 20 years! The process ranges from $34 for 750mL, $24 for 375mL and $14 for the 200mL format.

We brought back four bottles which I intend to slip into blind tastings so see if anyone can guess what the wine is. I'll lay odds nobody does. Unless they read this.

DOM'S PLĖNETUDE

Over my career as a wine writer I've had the pleasure and privilege of tasting some venerable wines and none more exciting than old champagne.

In 1976 I visited Moët & Chandon and was given a glass of the legendary 1911vintage by the Comtesse de Maigret. It had been disgorged that morning to impress a group of visiting English wine merchants and I was lucky enough to have what was left in the bottle.

The wine had lost its bubbles, but it tasted like a beautifully mature Meursault. I had no idea that champagne could last that long. It was explained to me that as long as the wine remained in contact with its lees, the ageing process is very slow.

So it was with great anticipation that I went to the Trump Hotel in Toronto last November to meet Richard Geoffroy, Dom Pérignon's chef de cave, to be introduced to a champagne simply called Dom Pérignon P2 1998. P2 is short for Plénitude 2.

Richard Geoffroy started as a champagne-maker with Moët Chandon in 1990 and has made 16 vintages of the company's prestige cuvée, Dom Pérignon. He and his cellar staff discovered over the years that there were certain stages in the evolution of a vintage champagne left on its lees when it changes character. They called these passages *plénitudes* (completeness) and they determined that there were three of them in the life of a champagne.

The first *plénitude* for the 1998 vintage was in 2004 - which is the usual amount of time that Dom Pérignon spends on its lees before it is released for sale the following year. The time on the lees for Dom is twice as long as the regulations require. The wine I was about to taste was the same 1998 vintage held on its lees for fifteen years.

The 1998 vintage was a warm year and in describing it Geoffroy couldn't help resorting to a flight of poetry. The character of the vintage, he said, 'shows in aromatics beyond the silver character of iodine and smoke, the sheer ripeness of the fruit. The richness comes from the ripeness of the fruit.'

At noon – an excellent time for champagne; but then again what time isn't? - we tasted Dom Pérignon P2 together. Not out of flutes shaped like cows' udders, which I was expecting, but served in wine glasses that looked like the Riedel Chardonnay stem. Geoffroy gave up using flutes 15 years ago because, he says, 'they don't do justice to the wine.'

Well, I'm here to tell you that P2 is magnificent, pure and precise with a creaminess in mid-palate and a life-giving spine of lemony acidity. The wine is amazingly young both in its visual appearance and on the palate: or as Geoffroy put it, 'bafflingly youthful, rather insolent in a way.'

The third Plénitude, says Geoffroy, will have been left on its lees for '35 to 40 years.'

If you're thinking you can replicate the Plénitude concept in your home cellar by leaving a bottle of champagne for seven or fifteen years, forget it. In order to work its magic, the wine has to be resting on its lees. When you buy champagne, it has already been disgorged. The dead yeast cellars have been removed, first by riddling the bottles until the sediment rests on the crown caps; then the necks are immersed in a freezing solution. When opened, the pressure of the gas ejects a plug of ice containing the yeast residue leaving a clean wine. The bottle is then topped up with sweetened wine to create the house style. Or unsweetened wine for Brut Zero.

If you're asking what the cost of P2 is you probably can't afford it. Neither can I. It will retail for about twice the price of the current vintage of Dom Pérignon. I just hope I'll be around to sample P3 though.

WINE NOVA SCOTIA STYLE

When Life gives you lemons, goes the old saw, make lemonade.

When Nature gives you an overabundance of acidity in your grapes and you're a wine region, what do you do? Well, you play to your strengths and make fresh sparkling and white table wines that pair so well with the wealth of seafood around your coastline.

That's the philosophy that will turn Nova Scotia into the next darling of sommeliers looking for something new to offer their clientele.

Recently I spent six days touring the wineries of the Annapolis and Gaspereau Valleys and the Malagash Peninsula. What I tasted convinced me that some of the best sparkling wines currently made in Canada are being produced in a province that is, famously, midway between the Equator and the North Pole.

Nova Scotia vintners respect the traditional Champagne blend of Chardonnay and Pinot Noir, but they are also pressing into service their own local varieties, such as L'Acadie, Vidal and Seyval Blanc.

The first signal that something special was going on here was seven years ago when I visited Benjamin Bridge in the Gaspereau Valley. In keeping with the new wave of Canadian wineries, Benjamin Bridge's owner Gerry McConnell made his fortune in another field (mining) before getting his feet into the vat, as it were. Given Nova Scotia's climate, he wisely decided to concentrate on sparkling wines, but he set his sights ambitiously high. McConnell wanted to make sparkling wine up to the standard of Champagne's Grandes Marques; and if he couldn't do it he would abort the project.

To realize his dream, in 1999, he purchased a 50-acre property with its 1845 Westcott family barn and did an initial vineyard planting of 10-acres. He then hired consultant Peter Gamble, the founding executive director of Ontario's Vintners Quality Alliance. When McConnell shared his vision with Gamble, the former winemaker for Hillebrand suggested that if you want to rival champagne you have to get a Champenois winemaker on board - which is exactly what McConnell did.

The late oenologist Raphael Brisbois, a former *chef de cave* at Piper Heidsieck, who had created India's celebrated sparkling wine, Omar Khayyam, as well as consulting to California's Iron Horse, Mount Dome in Washington and Blue Mountain Vineyards in BC.

Together with Gamble, the pair started experimenting with sparkling blends in 2002, using Pinot Noir, Chardonnay, Vidal and Nova Scotia's signature white grape L'Acadie. Gerry McConnell had given Brisbois and Gamble carte blanche to leave the wines on their lees as long as they wanted – an invitation that would make any bank manager cringe.

Ten years later Peter Gamble held a blind tasting in Toronto's toney Canoe restaurant for sommeliers and wine writers, pitting two of Benjamin Bridge's 2004 bubblies against the likes of David Léclapart L'Apôtre Blanc de Blancs 2005 and - here's where the real chutzpah comes in – and Roederer Cristal 2004, which at the time was the champagne of choice of Hip Hop artists, selling for $289 a bottle.

Interestingly, the grape blend in the Benjamin Bridge wines would make a traditional Champenois shudder – 57% Pinot Noir, 22% Chardonnay, 15% the hybrid Vidal, and 6% of the local Nova Scotia variety, L'Acadie. (Since 2009 Benjamin Bridge`s sparkling wines *en tirage* have been 100% vinifiera.)

So, there we were, 18 sommeliers and wine writers, with four glasses of bubbly in front of us, two champagnes and two Benjamin Bridge sparklers. Their color didn't give anything away, nor did the activity of the mousse, nor the size of the bubbles. It would be all in the taste to determine which were champagnes and which were the Nova Scotia sparklers. My notes at the time read:

Wine #1: Bready, leesy nose; rich, green nut flavor, crisply dry, good length, mature apple flavor on the finish. Very champagne-like. 91 points.

Wine #2: Leesy, bready nose with lemony, floral and honey notes; very elegant, light and crisp on the palate. Delicious. Probably Cristal. 93 points

Wine #3: Earthy, apple and lemon flavors, mature notes, with a touch of sweetness in mid palate. Late Disgorged? 90 points

Wine # 4: Minerally, crisply dry, green apple, lemony, very fresh and lingering. Likely BB. 91 points.

When the dust settled the majority of the tasters placed Wine #2 as their favorite wine. The serving order was:

1. David Léclapart L'Apôtre Blanc de Blanc 2005 ($138)
2. Benjamin Bridge Brut Reserve 2004 ($74)
3. Roederer Cristal 2004 ($289)
4. Benjamin Bridge Brut Reserve 2004 Late Disgorged ($89.50)

And what does this prove? a) Nova Scotia has the climate and soil to make world-class sparkling wines. b) It pays to hire experts, and c) ultimately, I'm a cheap date. My preference was for the least expensive bubbly.

And Benjamin Bridge is not the only winery making great sparkling wine in Nova Scotia. If you visit, don't miss Grand Pré Vintage Brut 2009; from the province's newest winery, Lightfoot & Wolfville Sparkling 2013 and Blomidon Estate Winery Woodside Road Vineyard Sparkling Brut 2011.

And then there is Nova Scotia's unique appellation for white wines that express the terroir of the region, called Tidal Bay. But that's another story...

EARLY WARNING FOR GRAPE GROWERS

This past winter has been one of the coldest that grape growers in Ontario have suffered in the past 30 years. Unrelenting polar temperatures have put their vines at risk.

But the 2015 harvest may well have been saved by the intervention of Brock University's Cool Climate Oenology and Viticulture Institute's VineAlert program.

VineAlert, according to Brock's press department, 'tracks a grape bud's ability to survive severe cold during the dormant season from October to April, signaling at what temperature different varieties would sustain damage.'

An economic impact study suggests that VineAlert helps Ontario's grape industry avoid up to $12.8 million in lost sales from a single severe cold weather event, as well as $11.7 million in lost sales while damaged vines recover in subsequent years, and $29.1 million in vine renewal and replacement costs.

VineAlert warns growers by email when extreme weather events are about to happen. This information allows the growers to make vineyard management decisions - when to switch on their expensive wine machines or to hire helicopters to hover over the vineyard to warm the air at vine level and avoid crop loss. (The draught from a helicopter's blades pulls down the slightly warmer air layered above the vineyard, allowing it to circulate amongst the vines thus reducing the possibility of frost damage. Helicopters can protect a vineyard of up to 50 acres against frost damage at one session.).

Currently some 300 Ontario growers are signed up for the VineAlert program - which is currently free – and they receive emails when severe cold weather threatens. In addition, the program provides specific information for different micro-climates within a single Ontario region. For instance, say, Riesling on the Beamsville bench.

VineAlert also informs growers at what temperature different varieties are able to tolerate cold weather based on their location and stage of dormancy.

According to CCOVI's Dr. Jim Willwerth, who is the lead scientist on the project, 'There is no other program that monitors so many varieties and regions. We are also the only one to have a dedicated web database of information that seamlessly transfers the information to the grower.'

Dr. Willwerth has tested almost every vinifera that has been planted in Ontario and has concluded that the most susceptible varieties to winter kill are Nebbiolo and Barbera; but in terms of the most commonly planted vinifera, the most sensitive are Semillon, Sauvignon Blanc, Merlot and Syrah. The hardiest vinifera is generally Riesling. 'Things like crop levels can also impact hardiness,' says Dr. Willwerth, 'but in general Riesling is pretty tough in terms of vinifera and isn't that picky in terms of site or crop level.'

The research into varietal cold-hardiness has another economic benefit. Growers, nurseries and wineries are using the data to help decide what to plant and on what site. And what particular clones are best suited to specific locations within Ontario.

In addition to the VineAlert program, Dr. Willwerth's team at CCOVI have instituted a grape pre-harvest monitoring program through which they track five varieties across the Niagara Region for grape maturity leading up to harvest. 'We plan on doing a similar program called TanninAlert,' says Dr. Willwerth, 'where we provide tannin maturity for red cultivars to help understand Ontario tannin composition/quality and how vintages are impacting them. This will help provide advice for red wine making.'

COOVI has been working very closely with researchers in British Columbia at Agriculture and Agri-Food Canada Summerland. The Institute also has a network of cold hardiness researchers across North America, including scientists from New York, Washington State, Oregon, Colorado, Idaho, Michigan, California and Virginia. 'We have been doing joint trials and are working towards larger collaborations. I also have colleagues in Quebec and Nova Scotia who have interest in cold hardiness work. I have been contacted by people in Rioja, Chile and other regions about our program and how wind machines work. They have had freeze injury in recent years.'

So, we're not the only ones who endure frigid winters.

FINDING A SENSE OF PLACE

If you're a Burgundian Pinot Noir nut you've probably already done this: driven the 60-kilometre Route des Grands Crus from Santenay to Dijon. If you have, you'll have navigated the world's greatest wine list.

The route takes you through the vineyards of the Côte de Nuits and the Côte de Beaune (collectively known as the Côte d'Or – the world's most expensive agricultural real estate), as well as the lesser-known and less costly Hautes-Côtes in the hills above Route Nationale 74.

In the twelfth century Cistercian monks worked the land around Citeaux Abbey, now the spiritual home of Burgundy's wines. Their vineyard, within the walls of the monastery's 125-acre property, became Clos de Vougeot, the largest single vineyard in the Côte de Nuits. Over the generations the monks and local landowners found that certain sites produced better wines than others and they began to isolate these parcels.

In 1855, the same year that Bordeaux wines were classified into five growths on the basis of quality and price, Dr. Jules Lavalle published a topographical map of Burgundy's Côte d'Or. He detailed every vineyard from Santenay to Dijon and rated them in quality terms as *Hors ligne, Tête de Cuvée, Première, Deuxième* and even *Troisième Cuvée*.

This system, simplified and formalized by the Beaune Committee of Agriculture in 1861, became the appellation contrôlée system for the Côte d'Or that was given the stamp of law in 1936. Today, every vineyard in Burgundy is stratified within a pyramid of quality - from grand cru at the top, descending through premier cru, to village wine, down to generic Bourgogne.

And what makes one vineyard better than another and worthy of being a grand cru rather than a premier cru? The French have a word for it – *terroir*.

Terroir is the sum of three things – what happens to a vine above the ground, below the ground and the way it is tended. This quasi-mystical concept involves the nature of the soil, the drainage, the vine's exposure to sunlight, how it is trellised and pruned and what happens to the grapes once they enter the cellar. In a word, *terroir* is 'a sense of place.'

Terroir, as every Burgundy aficionado knows, can make wines from adjacent plots taste discernibly different. Think Volnay and Pommard, the elegance of the former and the power of the latter, and yet they are neighboring villages.

The winemaker in Ontario who best exemplifies the exploitation terroir is Thomas Bachelder. Bachelder made wine in Burgundy and Oregon before settling in Ontario to make Chardonnay and Pinot Noir for Le Clos Jordanne. At Le Clos he produced a series of single vineyard wines that were a true expression of the soil in which they were grown.

He now makes wine under the Bachelder label in all three regions as well as overseeing the cellar at a new Niagara winery called Domaine Queylus. A Pinot Noir specialist, Bachelder says, 'Pinot Noir is one of the best grapes for expressing terroir. Chardonnay does it well, Riesling does it well, but Pinot Noir is more transparent, the terroir shines through it.' *(Thomas Bachelder now has his own label and makes Chardonnay and Pinot Noir from specific parcels within several vineyards*.)

If you want an object lesson in the effects of terroir in Ontario, taste side by side two Pinot Noir wines from Coyote's Run in Niagara-on-the-Lake: Red Paw and Black Paw are two contiguous vineyards. The age of vines are the same; the mix of clones is the same; the wines are made in the same fashion but the flavor profiles are totally different.

I asked the winery's then owner Jeff Aubrey what accounted for the distinctive taste profiles?

‘In a word,’ he said, ‘soils. Red Paw is iron rich, hard and stony, well drained with low organic content. Technically, it’s called the Trafalgar series of silty clay which is quite red because of the iron. Black Paw (which abuts Red Paw) is Toledo series of silty clay loams, formed from the muck on the lakebed of the former Lake Iroquois that covered most of southern Ontario millions of years ago. The soil is remarkably dense, heavy blue clay. There’s lots of organic matter which holds moisture. Black Paw delivers darker fruit flavors because the heat capacity causes the soil to stay warmer longer into the fall period. This makes for riper grapes, even though the Brix levels (sugar readings) and acids are the same as Red Paw. Red Paw, on the other hand has an amazing perfume year after year. One wine is feminine, the other is masculine.’

The LANGUAGE OF WINE

Whenever I conduct a wine tasting I invite the participants to ask questions. In order to make the guests feel comfortable about speaking out in public I try a little humor. I say, 'Please feel free to ask questions at any point. Remember, there are no dumb questions about wine...(pause)...Apart from one. I was once asked, "Should I swallow my gum before I taste?"'

Now, there is no real answer to that one, except perhaps, 'Stick it behind your ear. Why break the habit of a lifetime.' But the point is that we wine writers are generally guilty of a presumption of knowledge on the part of our audience – a failing of most academics who have spent years studying their particular discipline and developed a coded vocabulary that excludes the uninitiated. We tend to assume basic information when faced by an enthusiastic audience who is willing to absorb, not only the wines in front of them, but what we have to say about those wines.

When we declare with authority that we can smell aromas of peach and green pineapple in the bouquet of this Chardonnay it's not too far-fetched for someone, if they are brave enough, to put up their hand and ask, 'Do winemakers really add peaches and pineapples to their wine?' This is not an unreasonable question from someone who has never visited a winery or seen how wine is made.

As wine writers we have an obligation to communicate on various levels to wine lovers, whether they're attending their very first tasting or have a wine cellar that we would envy. Not everyone reads Wine Spectator, Decanter and Quench from cover to cover. There are degrees of enthusiasm for the fermented grape and we, as educators, must keep telling ourselves that not everyone is a future candidate for Master of Wine studies. Some just want to find a tasty wine that will be delicious with the roast chicken they're having that night.

I don't think of myself as a wine critic, rather as a wine evangelist; because I want to share my passion for wine which I believe to be the most civilized and civilizing of beverages that not only has health-giving benefits and sensory delights but can elevate the flavor of food as it elevates the conversation around the dinner table.

Ultimately, it all comes down to one's ability to communicate that passion.

My colleague and friend Tim Hanni, who is a trained chef as well as being the co-first American Master of Wine (the other was Joel Butler), is also a master communicator. While his peers might turn their noses up at White Zinfandel, Tim championed this pink confection since it introduced a generation to wine just as Mateus Rosé and Liebfraumilch had done before it.

Tim recognized the fact that when people tasted a wine for the first time, they either liked it or they didn't. They might not be able to parse its bouquet and deconstruct its flavors, but they had a definite opinion. So, (as mentioned in an earlier chapter) he coined the terms 'Yum' and 'Yuck' - a thumbs-up or thumbs-down as a tasting response.

This may seem overly simplistic, but it allowed the consumer to express a personal judgement on the wine without having to justify that opinion in the language of wine magazines which they did not understand. (Sometimes I'm flummoxed by some critics' descriptors.)

RISING WITH THE TIDE

The tasting room and retail stop at Avondale Sky in Nova Scotia measures 40 feet at the peak of its steeply-raked roof to a footprint of 36 by 50 feet.

Not the sort of dimensions one would normally associate with a winery. But the 1837 Carpenter Gothic-style building began life as a church – and not in its current location.

It was, in fact, the church's second move. The winery's website tells this story: 'The village of Walton had developed closer to the waterfront than was originally anticipated. So, one winter about a century and a half ago, the parishioners used oxen to move the building to its new site three kilometers from the old.'

In 2011 Stewart Vassalo and Stewart Creaser purchased St. Matthew's Church for $1.67 – the same price its congregation paid for the building in 1844. The couple had the deconsecrated church lifted off its foundations and ferried 42 kilometers down the Minas Basin shore to Newport. Had they not rescued it the church would have been torched so that the local fire brigade could practice their fire-fighting skills. The move took just over 24 hours, the stately church riding Minas Bay's perilous tides that rise and fall 42 feet.

This was not the first of the owners' efforts to preserve heritage buildings; Avondale Sky's fermentation tanks are housed in a 1920s hay barn they had salvaged from a dike along the St. Croix River ten kilometers from their vineyard.

Today Avondale Sky's winemaker Ben Swetnam produces a range of wines from Nova Scotia's signature white grape, L'Acadie, as well as a product conforming to the province's unique appellation, Tidal Bay.

The concept, launched with the 2012 vintage, was for wineries to produce a dry or off-dry white blend of locally grown grapes that speak to Nova Scotia's terroir. The primary grapes which make a majority of the blend have to be chosen from L'Acadie, Vidal, Seyval and Geisenheim 318 or a combination thereof. Secondary grapes, if used, can include Riesling, Chardonnay, Pinot Blanc and Pinot Gris and 11 other lesser varieties.

Then there is a third option of grapes for inclusion in the blend - aromatic varieties such as Gewurztraminer, Perle of Csaba, Traminette or New York Muscat, but only up to 15% of the total. Yields are regulated and no more than 20% new oak can be used, although stainless steel is recommended to maintain the freshness of the wines and their lightness (alcohol levels should not exceed 11%. Some are as low as 9.5%). Residual sugar must not climb above 20 grams per liter. Twenty grams per liter may sound high but given the exuberant acidity in Nova Scotia's grapes it makes for a more balanced wine.)

To ensure vintners respect the guidelines, the wineries have to submit their blends to a tasting panel of experts to ensure typicity. Currently 12 of the province's producers make a Tidal Bay wine.

I tasted all twelve at the launch of this year's Tidal Bay wines in Halifax in June. While stylistically they ranged from bone dry (Benjamin Bridge, Gaspereau Vineyards, Blomidon Estate, and Lightfoot & Wolfville, the province's newest winery opened this summer) to off-dry (Grand Pré, Luckett Vineyards, Mercator, Jost, Ste. Famille, Planters Ridge and, Annapolis Highland Vineyards) they all had a floral or aromatic component and were immensely drinkable.

Avondale Sky's Tidal Bay 2014 was a blend of L'Acadie, Vidal, Geisenheim 318, Minnesota Muscat and a variety I had never come across before, Petite Milo. The wine was pale straw in color with a Sauvignon Blanc-like nose, offering dry, gooseberry, green plum and cut grass flavors. Winemaker Ben Swetnam calls his wine, irreverently, 'Tiddly B.'

OLD WORLD VINTNERS, ANCIENT WORLD METHODS

Everything old is new again. Wine and winemaking may seem impervious to change but the industry is as susceptible to the whims of fashion as are the hemlines of women's skirts. And many vintners around the world are reverting back to the antediluvian origins of winemaking.

The first evidence that Stone Age man made wine from grapes was found as pits in pottery shards during archeological digs in Georgia near Mount Ararat (where Moses is presumed to have planted the first vineyard after the Flood). The shape of those pits suggested that they were not wild grapes but had been domesticated and grown specifically for the purpose of making wine. Carbon dating placed the pits back in time to 7000 BC.

Neolithic winemakers would have fermented their grapes in clay pots which they would bury in the ground and seal the aperture with mud. In Georgia they are making wine that way to this day; and now the rest of the wine world is beginning to take notice. Call it the Natural Wine movement - no additives, no sulphur, no artificial yeasts. On the island of Corsica, Yves Canarelli at Clos Canarelli is an ardent champion of this style of winemaking. 'The amphora protects the wine from oxidation in a natural way,' he says. 'I do not need to add any sulfur. The porous clay protects, the wine does not oxidize.'

Josko Gravner, in the Italy's northern province of Friuli-Venezia Giulia, uses huge bee's wax-lined amphorae buried in the ground to make both his red and white wines. Arianna Occhipinti, the young winemaker at Azienda Agricola Cos in the south-eastern tip of Sicily, uses 250 and 400 litter amphorae for her acclaimed wine 'Pithos' (Greek for a large storage container, which was another historical use for amphorae). On the west side of Sicily, Frank Cornelissen makes a red wine from the indigenous Nerello Mascalese grapes from the slopes of Mount Etna, called, appropriately enough, Magma.

Inspired by the Sicilian wines they tasted in 1999, Alain Viret and his son Philippe, proprietors of Domaine Viret at St. Maurice sur Eygues in the southern Rhône Valley, began making wine in clay amphorae too, a method that harmonized with their desire to produce biodynamic wines.

If you want to see how wine was made in Roman times you can visit Castello di Lispida near Padua, a former monastery now a hotel where they make wine in buried terracotta amphorae and in open wooden vats. Other notable European producers who have switched from stainless steel tanks to clay vessels are Elisabetta Foradori in Italy's Trentino Alto Adige (who has 70 amphorae); Luigi Tecce in Campania; Adega José de Sousa in Portugal's Alentej region; Marino Markezic in Croatia and Austria's Winzerhof Franz Landauer-Gisperg and Ploder Rosenberg.

And not only winemakers in the Old World are going back to the ancient methods of fermentation. Last October the Okanagan Valley's Laughing Stock Vineyards imported two amphorae from Italy. The first wine to be produced in these clay vessels will be a blend of Viognier, Roussanne and Marsanne.

Recently, I was in Chile and visited the De Martino winery in Isla de Maipo. The first thing that winemaker Marco De Martino showed me, with great pride, was his amphorae cellar. He has collected 156 amphorae that he purchased from local farmers and is currently producing a range of wines called Viejas Tinajus ('Old Jars').

Another aspect of a return to bygone technologies I noticed when touring Chilean wineries is a move away from stainless steel fermentation tanks to the same method used by the ancient Romans - cement tanks. Stainless steel tanks are inert which means there is no oxygen exchange and the fermentation temperature has to be regulated by cooling. Cement tanks are porous and allow the wine to breathe, making for a slow, gradual fermentation; and the volume of wine maintains a lower temperature. Vivianne Navarette, the winemaker at Viña Leyda in Chile's coastal region of the same name, says fermentation in cement tanks is particularly good for Pinot Noir.

Continuing on this theme of reinventing the wheel, if you thought that foot-treading grapes went out with Lucille Ball, you'd be very much mistaken. Virtually all the best vintage ports are still pressed by foot and more and more table wine producers are reverting to it. In California alone, Arnot-Roberts, Wind Gap, A Donkey and Goat, Core Wine Company, Donelan Family Wines, Neyers Vineyards, Morelet Family Vineyards, Old World Winery, Clos Mimi and Joseph Swan Vineyards all put their foot in it.

The human foot is, in fact, the ideal tool to crush grapes. The naked sole is firm enough to break the skins of grapes and squeeze the pulp but malleable enough not to crush the pits and stalks that contain harsh, bitter tannins. And the heat of the human leg warms up the must (the crushed berries) and helps the fermentation to start. (But I'm here to tell you – food-treading is damned hard work.)

In wine and in life it seems there is no substitute, for the wisdom of the ages and its accumulated experience.

A PASSION FOR WINE

If you love wine and you want to visit Montreal, take my advice and go in November. November is the most wine-soaked month in the calendar there.

Several years ago, the SAQ took a look at all the major wine events that happened in the city over the year and decided to concentrate them in the month of November. Playing off 'Happy Christmas,' they called it 'Joyeux Novembre.'

Kicking off the month is a three-day event called 'Passion Vin' which is centered at the Hotel Bonaventure. Passion Vin celebrates its 15th anniversary this year (2016).

Then there's a tasting at Bonsecours Market of the association of private wine importers whose unwieldy acronym is RASPIPAV. (Some 16,000 wines are privately imported into Quebec as opposed to the 8,000 skus offered by Quebec's provincial liquor outlets, the SAQ.)

The next November offering is the two-day, themed La Grande Dégustation de Montréal in Place Bonaventure that features more than 200 winemakers, distillers and brewers from around the world (this past year's theme was **S**pain**,** Grenache and global bubblies).

Then comes La Grande Tablée, a one-night dinner at the Fairmount Queen Elizabeth Hotel with menus created by Quebec's top chefs. Some 700 gourmets attend. And finally, at the end of the month, there's a three-day celebration of the wines and cheese of Quebec at Bonsecours Market.

But the most intriguing event is Passion Vin. Martin Gautier, president of the organization for the past four years, told me that wineries who accept the invitation at attend must provide 36 bottles of each of six vintages. Plus, they are expected to donate bottles for the live and silent auctions that take place during the Grand Banquet on the final night - and supply wine for this dinner.

I attended Passion Vin this past November and, just to get you salivating, here's a line-up of the tastings, all conducted by the owners and professionally served by a group of some 30 sommeliers who volunteered their time: six vintages of Louis Roederer Cristal Brut (2006, 2005, 2004, 2002, 2000 and 1999) followed by a four-course lunch at which five wines from Domaine du Pégau Châteauneuf du Pape were served – their 2014 white and four vintages of the red wine (2012, 2011, 2008 and 2009).

In the afternoon, a tasting of six vintages of Col d'Orcia Brunello di Montalecino (2001, 2004, 1997, 1990, 1977 and 1968). Then six vintages of Vieux Château Certan (2012, 2010, 2009, 2008, 2005, 1998).

The next morning, a tasting of six wines from Jean-Claude Boisset, introduced by winemaker Grégory Patriat – Beaune Les Vignes Franche 2012, Puligny-Montrachet 2011, Corton Charlemagne 2011 and three vintages of Clos de la Roche (2011, 2012 and 2008). This was followed by a lunch tasting of five wines from the Piemonte producer Ceretto - an Arneis 2014, a Barolo 2010, Barolo Bricco Rocche 2008, Barolo Cannubi San Lorenzo 2005, and Barolo Bricco Rocche Brunante 1999.

After lunch a tasting of Château Troplong Mondot 'Mondot' 2011 (the second wine), and Château Troplong Mondot vintages 2011, 2006, 2004, 1998 and 2010.

Before the Grand Banquet that evening there was a Roederer Champagne reception followed by a five-course meal that book-ended a live auction. During the bidding the winery owners who had donated the bottles would leap up on stage to outdo each other by adding visits, meals and overnight stays to their lots.

The combined live and silent auctions on that night raised $1,041,907. These proceeds will go to the construction of an integrated cancer center of Montreal's Maisonneuve-Rosemount Hospital. The Quebec government has said that if the wine enthusiasts of Montreal raise $12,000,000, they would match the amount to finance the construction of the new center.

All it takes is wine to open people's hearts - and wallets.

CANADA'S SIGNATURE GRAPES?

In the international world of wine, red hybrids such as Baco Noir and Maréchal Foch have the appeal of a tag-team wrestling bout.

They are the blue-collar grapes, the early-ripening, winter-hardy, heavy-bearing hybrids that lack the finesse, the breed and the delicate dispositions of Old Europe's noble vinifera varieties. (You know these as Pinot Noir, Cabernet Sauvignon, Merlot, et al.)

Yet the contemporary Canadian wine industry owes Baco and Foch more than a debt of gratitude, because they replaced the unlamented Concord and other labrusca varieties that made our wines undrinkable. And today producers such as Henry of Pelham, Malivoire, Quails' Gate and Summerhill have produced cult wines from these trailer park varieties that can cost as much as their continental cousins.

Their story goes back to 1946, when Brights' winemaker Adhemar de Chaunac brought back from France 40 European vine varieties including a crossing bred in Alsace called Kuhlmann 188-2. The grape was subsequently renamed Maréchal Foch after the French World War I general.

In those years Ontario's Horticultural Research Institute recommended growers plant Foch and other hybrids such as Baco Noir, Chelois, Léon Millot and Seibel 9549 (the latter would be renamed De Chaunac to honor the pioneer of the Ontario industry), the theory being these early ripening hybrids would survive the winter better than the delicate, finicky viniferas.

Today, Foch and Baco (one of whose parents is Folle Blanche – a Cognac grape) are the only red hybrids consistently used to make varietal wines in Ontario and British Columbia.

Flash back to 1974, the year Donald Ziraldo and the late Karl Kaiser got their manufacturing permit to produce up to 10,000 gallons of wine.

'In reality,' Kaiser recalled, 'we made about 3,500 gallons (1600 cases) of a wine we called Vin Nouveau. It was made to a large extent from De Chaunac, part was Chelois and part Maréchal Foch. We also had been given three 500-litre barrels by the LCBO in which I fermented straight Maréchal Foch, approximately 160 cases.'

The following year Inniskillin got its winery license, but not before the neophyte vintners thought that Labatt's had pulled the rug out from under their fledgling enterprise. The owners of Château-Gai placed a print ad featuring their then winemaker Paul Bosc walking through a vineyard. The copy line announced that the winery was introducing a wine called Maréchal Foch 'and better things to come.'

In December 1975, The Globe & Mail put on a blind tasting at which Inniskillin Maréchal Foch 1974 bested a noted Beaujolais, Château de la Ferrière Brouilly 1973.

'The six tasters had to do a re-tasting,' laughs Ziraldo, 'because they thought it was impossible for a Canadian wine to beat out a named-village wine from Beaujolais.'

Quails' Gate is one of several wineries in BC that produce Maréchal Foch, and the most ambitious, making three different wines from this grape – a Limited Release Old Vines Foch, a Family Reserve Old Vines Foch and a fortified port-style wine called F.V.F. (Fortified Vintage Foch) – which account for almost 7 per cent of the winery's production. Other Okanagan producers of Foch include Hubertus, Lang, Sperling, Summerhill, House of Rose, Recline Ridge and Niche Wine Company, as well as Muse Winery on Vancouver Isle which calls their wine Risqué Rouge.

Alderlea Vineyards, also on Vancouver Island, has a proprietary label called "Clarinet" (100% Foch) which sells out as soon as it hits the shelves.

At Henry of Pelham in the Niagara Peninsula, the former winemaker Ron Giesbrecht established a cult following for the winery's Baco Noir which first appeared on the market in 1988. He tells the story of pouring his Baco Noir Reserve at Vinexpo in Bordeaux several years ago: a Loire vintner who used to grow this variety before it was outlawed in France recoiled in horror when he saw the label. A rather animated discussion ensued until he finally agreed to taste the wine.

'The smile on his face and the appreciation he expressed,' says Giesbrecht, 'was as much of a surprise to me as it was to him. That experience told me two important things: even entrenched prejudices can be overcome when the wine is good, and secondly, that Baco does not display a pleasing character in all places – so our site is suited to the grape.'

Currently Henry of Pelham's winemaker Sandrine Bourcier is continuing the tradition of making sterling Baco Noir. (Lawrence Buhler, H of P's current winemaker, is also a dab hand at Baco Noir.)

When handled well, both Baco and Foch can make complex wines, but they still suffer the stigma of their birth, and most winemakers look on these street fighters as inexpensive wines for blending to give depth of color and add acidity to the blend. It takes a leap of faith to put them through new barrels as a varietal wine.

Foch and Baco will always remain niche products but given the fact that Ontario growers have increased their plantings, it looks as if they're here to stay. And given the fact that wine regions around the world are re-discovering their historic indigenous varieties – to escape the tyranny of ubiquitous Chardonnay, Cabernet Sauvignon and Merlot – maybe there is another life for those much-maligned French hybrids.

FLIGHT FROM THE FLUTE

The universal symbol for champagne is the saucer-shaped glass. Even today when most of them have been relegated to the ice cream parlor.

The coupe was designed for Queen Victoria who found that the bubbles in champagne gave her flatulence. The purpose of the shallow shape is to help flatten the wine, i.e. to remove the bubbles the vignerons of Champagne had labored so long and lovingly to introduce into it.

Queen Victoria, having emasculated her champagne, used to add, heaven forbid, Lochnagar malt whisky to her claret thereby simultaneously ruining another two of the planet's outstanding alcoholic beverages.

To add insult to injury, one of her subjects invented the swizzle stick.

Think of a tiny umbrella frame whose spokes can slide into its handle. By opening it and twirling it in a champagne coupe you effectively kill the mousse.

Maybe that's why the French eventually adopted the elongated flute as the desired receptacle for champagne since the aperture is too small to accommodate a swizzle stick.

But the French have only themselves to blame for legitimizing the coupe as the *de rigeur* champagne glass. The cover of Patrick Forbes seminal book, ‘Champagne, The Wine, The Land and The People’ (published in 1997), bore the photo of a piece of Sèvres porcelain, molded, it is said, from Marie Antoinette’s left breast. Charming as that may be, champagne tastes better out of clear glass than out of a china bra. Just as it does from a glass rather than an actress’s slipper.

As we know the wheel of fashion turns inexorably and now champagne producers have shunned the cow’s udder-shaped flute in favor of a vessel usually reserved for white wines – a tulip-shaped glass, the better to appreciate the bouquet while still enjoying the display of the upward passage of the bubbles.

It was Richard Geoffroy, Dom Pérignon’s *chef de cave*, who alerted me to the trend when he served me his Dom Pérignon P2 1998 in what looked like a Riedel Chardonnay stem. Geoffroy gave up using flutes 16 years ago because, he says, ‘they don't do justice to the wine.’

So, what are we to do with all those flutes we’ve been using for champagne and carefully washing by hand all these years? Demote them to Prosecco?

Some years ago, I was involved in a tasting at Inniskillin to determine the ideal glass for Icewine. Georg Riedel, whose company produces glasses to enhance the flavor of just about every variety of wine, was commissioned to design the perfect Icewine glass. Our panel eventually settled on a design whose bowl starts in a V and then curves out into a tulip shape.

I had been a great fan of Riedel glasses ever since Robert Mondavi conducted a tasting of his wines using several glass shapes. Riedel won through in each trial.

Riedel's glasses for individual grape varieties were designed to deliver the wine precisely on the palate to emphasize its best qualities (as opposed to the *Les Impitoyables* line of glasses by Peugeot which 'intensify the characteristics of wine by enhancing their qualities or bringing out the slightest flaw.' Hence the name which translates as 'the Merciless Ones.'

And then, from a true believer I left the Riedel congregation when the company introduced the O series of tumblers - wine glasses without stems but each designed for a specific grape variety.

The first thing a wine lover learns is not to hold a glass by the bowl. Your body heat will warm up the wine and your fingers will leave prints on the glass. The rationale behind this 'innovation' was that these glasses are safer in the dishwasher.

But they do have one advantage over stemware. They float in hot tubs.

THE QUEEN WHO SHRUNK THE WINE CELLAR

Wine lovers, I have found, are unrepentant collectors, not only of bottles of wine but of all the paraphernalia that does along with wine - labels, corkscrews, corks and even those little metal discs under the cage of champagne bottle corks.

And, of course, wine books.

I must confess that I was an avid wine book collector until I moved into a condo and had to divest myself of some 700 volumes. It was like giving away children.

But there was one book I parted with years ago that I still think about as a bitter-sweet memory. It was the cellar book for Queen Mary's dolls' house at Windsor Castle. Its beige, hard cover carried the name, 'Berry Brothers & Rudd,' the renowned London-based wine merchant.

What I had found in a second-hand book shop in London was not the actual cellar-book. That one resides in the wine cellar of the dolls' house. It was the template that was used to miniaturise the volume to the size of a postage stamp - to be in perfect proportion (one inch to the foot) with all the other contents of what has been described as 'The world's largest and most beautiful dolls' house.'

The next time you have tea at Windsor Castle ask the Queen about her grandmother's palatial, four-storey dolls' house. She will tell you, no doubt, that it was designed in 1924 by the great British architect Sir Edwin Lutyens, who took time off from another project - building India's capital, New Delhi – to indulge the royal request.

Queen Mary, the wife of George V, was by all accounts a voracious and rapacious collector of miniatures. According to a contemporary, 'Her methods of collecting were notoriously ruthless: she would admire an object so relentlessly and so forcefully that its owner felt obliged to hand it over. Prudent hostesses hid their favorite things before she arrived.'

The fruits of Queen Mary's hyper-active collector gene can be seen in this most remarkable artefact. The dolls' house contains a host of miniature items that actually function: 'There are Purdey's shotguns that 'break and load' (and may even fire), monogrammed linens... electricity and lifts, a garage of cars with engines that run. It even has running water through its tiny pipes.'

Equally extraordinary is the wine cellar in the basement. The bottles are half an inch tall; each stoppered with cork and sealing wax and labelled with reproductions of real labels. They were filled with the actual wines – First Growths clarets and Montrachet. The Veuve Clicquot Champagne bottles each have their own straw sleeve – the old method of packaging champagne before moulded Styrofoam.

A book about the dolls' house gives this description of the contents of the wine cellar: 'The entire cellar amounts to 22 cases of Champagne, ten cases of claret, 14 cases of port, four cases of sherry, two cases of Madeira, four cases of white Burgundy, two cases of Sauternes, two cases of Graves, two cases of red Burgundy and two cases of hock; then it's on to brandy (four cases), gin (four cases), rum (one case) Scotch whisky (one quarter cask and 13 cases), Irish whiskey (ditto), French vermouth (two cases), Italian vermouth (two cases), liqueurs (seven cases) and beer (17 cases and two casks).'

Much of this inventory was hand-written into the cellar book that I had in my possession; and I wanted to find out if it was indeed the model for the Queen's dolls' house cellar book. So, some forty years ago, I took it down to Berry Brothers & Rudd, Britain's oldest wine merchant, at No. 3 St. James's Street. The facade of the building looks exactly as it must have looked when the store was opened by 'the Widow Borne' in 1698.

Inside, No. 3 has changed little since the widow opened her doors as a purveyor of coffee to the London clubs. The coffee scales and the mill are there still along with records of customers' weights spanning three centuries.

Anthony Berry, the then director, told me that the hand-written entries were made by his late father who had been commissioned by the Palace to lay down the cellar for the dolls' house. He eyed the volume with the same kind of naked desire that Queen Mary must have displayed when she happened upon a miniature that she wanted to add to her collection.

Looking around at this magnificent old building I thought that the cellar book really ought to be here in these historic surroundings – so I presented it to Anthony Berry.

Now Berry Brothers has a magnificent selection of old ports and I was thinking that he might just reward me with a bottle or two in exchange for my unique gift.

'Thank you, old boy,' he said to me. 'And I would like you to accept this.'

He reached behind him and took a book from the shelf. It was a history of No.3 St. James. He even signed it.

It was one of the wine books that I divested myself of when I moved to the condo.

DO YOU KMOW YOUR CAPITALS?

Can you name the only world capital that has commercial vineyards within its boundaries?

If you said Paris you'd be mistaken, although there is a single, tiny, enclosed vineyard on a north-facing slope in Montmartre planted to some 2,000 vines; but it's not a *commercial* vineyard.

The British novelist Julian Barnes described this tiny Parisian parcel in a travel piece he wrote for The Guardian newspaper: 'The Clos was created in 1933 by the city of Paris on what was previously, according to a municipal tin placard, "a waste land, the refuge of tramps and a playground for local children". There is a folkloric Fête des Vendanges each October (with the grapes pressed in the basement of the 18th arrondissement's *mairie*), whereupon the production of 1,000 or so bottles are auctioned (for charity).'

My London wine writer colleague Tim Atkin MW has tasted it twice and described it as 'somewhere between a decent Beaujolais and an Hautes Cotes de Nuit red – light, fruity and appealing, but of no great complexity.'

The correct answer to the capital question is Vienna. The city of *Sacher torte,* Gustav Klimt and horse-drawn carriages boasts 1,680 acres of vineyards within its limits. These vineyards support 630 producers - one for every 2,500 of its inhabitants. The vintners here grow mainly the Grüner Veltliner grape.

The district of Grinzing - a village that merged with Vienna in 1892 - is the home of *heurigen*, the traditional wine taverns that serve the new, still-fermenting Grüner Veltliner (the white equivalent of Beaujolais nouveau). Gustav Mahler is buried in Grinzing's cemetery and Beethoven lived here in 1817, the year he was commissioned by the London Philharmonic Orchestra to write his 9th Symphony. As a plaque on the wall attests, the composer stayed in a *heuriger* called Mayer am Pfarrplatz. Here I ate a meal that Beethoven himself must have enjoyed – schnitzel, wurst and sauerkraut with spaetzle and a glass of chilled Grüner Veltliner. Followed by a flaky pastry filled with what seemed like a half a pint of whipped cream.

The Grüner Veltliner grape, a cross between Traminer and St. Georgen, also known for some reason as Tarant Bily, represents 30 per cent of all white varieties planted in Austria; and while tourists drink it in heurigen as a frothy, cloudy wine when it's a matter of weeks' old, it can age magnificently.

At a celebration of the Salomon family's 222nd anniversary of the acquisition of their winery in Krems, I tasted their Grüners going back to 1971, 1964 and 1954. It truly is one of the world's great white wines and a highly versatile food wine.

In 2002, a seminal blind taste-off was held in London between Austrian Grüner Veltliner and Chardonnay and the world's most iconic Chardonnays from Burgundy, California, and Australia. Austrian wines trumped the field in all three categories outscoring such famous producers as Louis Latour (Burgundy), Angelo Gaja (Piemonte), Robert Mondavi (Napa), and Baron Thénard (Burgundy).

The top wine of the tasting was Knoll **Grüner Veltliner** 'Vinothekfüllung' **Smaragd** 1990 from Wachau, followed by Bründlmayer Grüner Veltliner 'Ried Lamm' 1997 from Kamptal.

I tasted wines from both these producers in June at Vienna's annual VieVinum wine festival and can attest to their excellent quality. At this three-day event, held in the baroque surroundings of the Hofburg Palace, I also tasted flights of Austrian red wines - three indigenous grape varieties, Zweigelt, Blaufränkisch and St. Laurent which are produced as mono-varietals or blended with Cabernet or Merlot.

While these wines showed some good pedigree, especially the Blaufränkisch, I was most impressed by a range of 28 Pinot Noir. Austrian producers of Pinot Noir to look for are, from Niederösterrich, Schloss Gobelsburg (who also make stunning Grüner Veltliner), Gerhard Morkowitsch and Kurt Angerer. From Burgenland, Kollwentz, Feiler-Artinger and Schloss Halbturn; from Thermenregion, Winzerhof Landauer-Gisperg; and from Wein (Vienna), Cobenzl and my top scoring wine of the five flights – Weininger Grand Select Pinot Noir 2011.

One of the most interesting wines I sampled over six days of tasting in Vienna was an amazingly fresh and lively rosé, Langmann Vulgo Lex Schilcher 2013.

I had never come across this wine before so I looked it up in Wikipedia: '...produced solely in the Austrian region of Western Styria ...The Schilcher wine itself is a distinct rosé made from the indigenous Blauer Wildbacher grape. It is a very old variety said to go back to the Celts, and manuscripts first record the name in the 16th century... Wines made from Wildbacher typically exhibit red berry and herbal flavors with a refreshing acidity. The color ranges from a light onion tinge to a deep ruby. The grape was once a wild variety which was said to contain alcohol compounds which, in turn, allegedly would induce wild inebriation, hence its colloquial name Rabiatperle – rabid pearl... Authentic Schilcher wine must carry the official emblem of the white horse (referring to the Lipizzans bred in Piber for the world-famous Spanish Riding School in Vienna)...'

Walking around Vienna there is no mistaking that this is a city of horses; and you don't need a well-trained nose to detect their omni-presence.

QUESTIONS FROM MY MAILBAG

Should I be concerned about the use of sulphur in winemaking?

Next time you pick up a bottle of wine have a look at the back label. It will probably include the warning: 'Contains Sulphites' (as well as injunction not to drink wine if you're pregnant).

Sulphur products are used in winemaking - especially at the time of bottling - as antioxidant and anti-bacterial agents, particularly for white wines. They are needed to stabilise color, keep the wine clean and give the product shelf-life.

But even wines that are made without recourse to sulphur will contain sulphites in some form. The reason is: the very act of fermentation actually creates sulphur dioxide, some of which will become bound into the wine. Even wines that have never been treated with sulphur will contain concentrations of up to 10 milligrams per litre of SO2. (The same is true, incidentally, for all foodstuffs that are fermented, such as cheeses and sauerkraut. And you can be sure that sulphur products are used to preserve the flavor and color in fresh fruits, dried fruits, vinegar, juices, soft drinks, sauces, beer - as well as wines.)

EU wine laws have come to terms with this irony by regulating that any wine with more than 10 milliliters per liter of sulphur dioxide must carry the warning that the wine contains sulphites.

Logically then, the back labels on wine bottles should read: not 'Contains Sulphites', but 'Guaranteed to Contain Sulphites.'

Most consumers can't sense the presence of sulphites on the nose or the palate at twice this level and it's only at above 30mg/l that experienced tasters can detect the 'burnt match head' odour that signals the presence of SO2. White, rosé and particularly sweet wines tend to have higher levels of bound-in sulphur than reds.

The World Health Organisation has set guidelines for the safe ingestion of sulphur dioxide, recommending a daily intake of no more than 0.7 grams per kilogram of body weight. For men of average weight this computes to less than a third of a bottle of a white wine with a concentration of 200 mg/l (the EU limit for dry white wine is 210mg/l – though these days this figure is very high given winemakers' desire to limit the amount of sulphites they use.).

Sulphur dioxide may cause allergic reactions in some people, especially if one suffers from asthma. Unfortunately, there is no way to tell the amount of SO2 in a given wine but there will always be some. And given modern winemaking techniques and the sensitivities winemakers have around the use of sulphur products - with the move to organic and biodynamic wine growing and cellar practices – there will continue to be less sulphites in wine.

Why does my face flush when I drink wine a glass of wine?

There are a few reasons: you could be reacting to the sulphites in the wine or to the alcohol – or you could have a medical condition known as rosacea. Alcohol makes the blood vessels expand and heavy drinking can cause a condition called *Alcohol Telangiectasia,* which manifests itself as broken capillaries rendered visible as a network of red spider veins.

Alcoholic flush happens to people who lack enough of the enzyme alcohol dehydrogenase (ADH) that converts alcohol to acetaldehyde. It's the accumulation of acetaldehyde that causes the flushing, usually accompanied by swelling of the skin, giddiness and headaches.

I have heard that taking heartburn remedies like Zantac or Pepcid before you ingest alcohol could alleviate the problem; and it could solve the problem of those who get headaches from the histamines in red wine. (I am no doctor, so consult your physician before taking any remedies if you're taking alcohol in any form.)

Rosacea is commonly found in fair-skinned people between the ages of 30 and 50 and is three times more common in women. Apart from environmental factors, facial flushing can be caused by stress, caffeine in tea and coffee, spicy foods, especially those high in histamines, and , of course, alcohol. While there is no cure as such the condition can be controlled with medical therapy and lifestyle changes. Rosacea sufferers can take cold comfort from the fact that they share the condition with former President Bill Clinton, the late Princess Diana, financier J.P. Morgan and the Dutch painter Rembrandt.

Will wine make me fat?

First, red wine is no more fattening than white wine. It's the amount of alcohol in conjunction with the residual sugar in the wine that determines the number of calories per glass. In determining the number of calories per pour a rough estimate is 25 calories for every 30 milliliters. So, the average bottle of wine will contain 650 calories. Sweet wines will be higher. A 6oz glass of dry red or white wine with 13% alcohol will contain up to 160 calories which is in the same ballpark as a generous slice of Madeira cake. So, the choice is yours. What's it to be? The wine or the cake?

BY ANY OTHER NAME

Every grape has its day, it seems. Each major variety is honored somewhere in the world with a festival or a competition.

The best known on this continent is Oregon's annual International Pinot Noir Celebration in McMinnville.

In Ontario we have the annual International Cool Climate Chardonnay Celebration for three days in July, known by its acronym, I4C. The original idea for Ontario winemakers was to spotlight Riesling but that variety had already been bagged by Chateau Ste. Michelle in Washington State. They call their event 'Riesling Rendezvous.'

Earlier this year I tasted a slew of wines in Toronto made from the Grenache grape as a prelude to a competition called 'Grenaches du Monde' which was held in a monastery in Zaragoza, Spain on February 5th.

The competition was open to all wines made from Grenache and its synonyms, Garnacha, Garnatxa and Cannonau. Some 600 wines from eight countries were entered in this year's competition.

Bon Apetit magazine called Grenache, 'the best grape you've never heard of,' although it's the second most widely-planted variety in the world. But you won't find it in Canada as the variety is a late-ripener and requires hot, dry growing conditions. That's why its natural habitat is Spain (where they call it Garnacha), Sardinia (Cannonau), California's San Joaquin Valley and Australia.

Barossa and McLaren Vale winemakers usually blend Grenache with Shiraz and Mourvèdre. They label this blend familiarly as GSM.

Perhaps Grenache is best known in the south of France where it's a major component of the Côtes du Rhône and Châteauneuf-du-Pape appellations (usually 80% of the blend, although Château Rayas famously makes their Châteauneuf from 100% Grenache). And of course, Grenache plays a major role in the rosés of Provence and the southern Rhône.

And being so widespread around the wine world, it's picked up more synonyms than a rock star at a beauty contest. Here are just some of them:
Granaccia, Lladoner, Tinto, Tinta, Carignan rosso, Carignane rousse, Tinto arogonese, Uva di Spagna, Sans Pariel, Tinto Menudo, Tinta Mencida, Tintilo de Rota, Roussillon, Roussillon Tinto Rouvaillard, Cannonau, Alicante, Rivesaltes and Redondal.

Being a hot- weather grape it accumulates a lot of sugar which in turn produces a high alcohol wine. Expect spicy, strawberry or raspberry notes in its flavor profile with a suggestion of white pepper. It tends to show a tawny hue at the rim as it ages - as a result of oxidation - developing tar or leather notes. That's why it's generally blended with Syrah, Carignan and Cinsault in southern France and Tempranillo in Spain.

As a result of its propensity to deliver high sugar levels, Grenache is used extensively in the production of fortified red wines such as Banyuls and the *vins doux naturel* wines of the Languedoc-Roussillon and Australia's Tawny.

Getting back to that pre-Grenaches du Monde tasting, our group was presented with ten wines.

Here are my top choices:

Tres Picos de Borsao Garnacha 2014 (Campo de Borga): Dense purple color; savory-herbal nose of red berries, black olives, spicy oak with a floral grace note; full-bodied, sweet, juicy black raspberry flavor; mouth-filling, well balanced carrying its 14.5% alcohol very well. (90.5)

Vieux Telegraphe Châteauneuf du Pape 2011 'Le Crau' (60% Grenache): mature ruby color; dry, savory nose of dried plums, licorice and pencil lead; full-bodied, dry, elegant and rich. Beautifully balanced with a bitter chocolate finish. (92)

Henschke Johann's Garden 2013 (60% Grenache with Shiraz and Mourvèdre): Dense purple color; smoky-herbal, blueberry nose; full-bodied, dry, blueberry flavor; firmly structured, spicy with lively acidity. (90)

Bodegas Alto Moncayo (Campo de Borga): dense purple-black color; spicy, strawberry and raspberry nose carried on oak notes; full-bodied, vanilla oak and well extracted red and black fruit flavors; fleshy and fruit-driven but finishes firmly. 16% alcohol. (92)

Pagos del Moncayo PdM Garnacha 2013 (Campo de Borga): dense purple-black color; smoky, herbal, pencil lead nose with spicy oak; elegant black fruits and black olive nose; full-bodied and juicy but finishes dry and firm. (90)

Bodegas Ruberte Tesor Garnacha 2013 (Campo de Borga): dense purple-black color; cedary, black cherry nose; full-bodied, elegant, rich blueberry flavor; beautifully balanced and seamless. (93)

MEN IN THE PINK

Each July for the past eight years (*in the 1990s*), restaurateur John Maxwell and wine scribe Billy Munnelly have hosted an event they call, 'Men in Pink.'

It's held at Allen's on Danforth Avenue in Toronto.

Allen's is Maxwell's funky bar and restaurant described by the owner on the website as a 'loving tribute to the Irish-American saloons of his native New York.'

'Men in Pink' is an al fresco lunch – not, as it might appear at first blush, a fund-raiser in aid of breast cancer, but a celebration of one of the most misunderstood and maligned beverages - rosé wine.

It's a men-only event and all the guests – usually around 50 – are required to dress in something pink. Ontario winemakers bring along bottles of their rosés which are copiously poured throughout a lunch whose courses are also pink in color.

This year the menu was Buttermilk beet and radish soup, barbecued smoked salmon, Barbecued Limousin Beef Tenderloin with a pink peppercorn and rosé sauce (served pink); and a dessert of Strawberry panacotta with fresh strawberries and orange sauce.

Probably more pink wine is consumed within four hours on those July days at Allen's than anywhere else on the planet.

'How Do You Get Bros to Drink Rosé Wine?' That was the headline of an article in Ad Weekly magazine published as recently as May of this year. Their advice: 'Package It Like It's Beer.'

Not that this pretty wine needs any such marketing machinations as the rosé category has been Number 1 with a bullet on liquor board charts - and around the world - for the last couple of years. Ontarians can choose from 164 rosés currently on LCBO shelves; Quebecers have even more - 187 at the SAQ; and in BC there are 128 skids at the BCLD.

There was a time when Real Men did not eat quiche or drink pink wine. But this is 2016 and real men wear pink and drink pink; although quiche, not so much.

Conspiracy theorists might ascribe the trend to a feminist plot to emasculate men; but the universal appeal of rosés, whether still or sparkling, has more to do, I believe, with a reaction to the heavy, densely colored, high alcohol wines of the New World, and the fact that rosés are not only the quintessential wine of summer but they're also versatile food wines.

Rosés are also inexpensive - apart from Domaine Ott's Château de Selle Coeur de Grain Rosé. Ontario's LCBO listed it at $46.95 which is more than double the price of the celebrity rosé Miraval owned by Brad Pitt and Angelina Jolie. Miraval looked like bargain by comparison at $22.95.
This wine is a partnership between the A-list couple and the Perrin family who own Château de Beaucastel in the Rhône. And then there is Domaine Tempier Bandol Rosé that sells in the US for $42; and the wine Forbes Magazine erroneously named as 'The World's Most Expensive Rosé' in March 2015: Caves d'Esclans Whispering Angel Rosé at $26.95.

What these four wines have in common is provenance: they all come from Provence, the spiritual home of rosé; and all, for the most part, are based on Grenache. And they are all virtually the same color – the palest rosés you will see. Flesh pink, in fact.

When it comes to choosing rosé the only thing you have to worry about is the sweetness level of the product. Many producers, especially in Canada, leave some residual sugar in their wines in the belief – mistaken as far as most wine lovers are concerned – that consumes expect a fruity sweetness in a pink wine.

Dry 'em out, I say, and make rosé a year-round wine rather than confining it to the sun-drenched days of summer.

THE BEST OF BUBBLES

Champagne may be the most frivolous of beverages but it`s also one of the most expensive, the most highly regulated in terms of its production, and the most difficult wine to make.

Just to set the record straight, champagne the drink, comes only from Champagne the region. All other sparklers, even those from Burgundy, Loire and Alsace are, by law, merely *vins mousseux*. The champagne houses are nothing if not litigious when it comes to protecting their appellation name - as the Ontario wine industry discovered in 1964 and again in 1987.

Champagne, apart from being the perfect aperitif, is also an indicator of the health of the global economy. Worldwide champagne sales set a record in 2007 at 339 million bottles. Following the 2008 bankruptcy of Lehman Brothers in the US, and its global consequences, demand dropped substantially. By 2009 sales were down by one million bottles. As first world economies rebounded in 2014 champagne sales were back to 304 million bottles.

The most expensive champagne is not Dom Pérignon - or any of the prestige cuvées of the other big producers - but Krug`s vintage-dated Clos d`Ambonnay Blanc de Noirs which has an average selling price in Canada of $2,953 a bottle. The wine comes from a half-acre, walled plot in the village of Ambonnay on the Montagne de Reims. And the average price of Krug`s Clos de Mesnil Blanc de Blancs (100% Chardonnay) in Canada is $1,256 a bottle. How would you like to find a brace of those in your Christmas stocking?

Within the boundaries of the Champagne appellation there are 319 villages, and each has been rated on a scale of 80% to 100%, based on the historic quality of the grapes grown there. There are 17 villages that are rated 100% by the *Comité Interprofessional des Vins de Champagne*, the region`s regulating body. And as such these villages have been accorded Grand Crus status. Ambonnay is one of them.

This rating determines the price of the wine and what percentage of that price goes to the growers. Some of the better-known 100% villages are Äy, Bouzy and Sillery for Pinot Noir and PInot Meunier (the two black grapes that go into the champagne blend) and Avize, Cramant and Le Mesnil for Chardonnay, the only white grape permitted in the region.

Slightly less exalted villages in terms of the quality of their grapes, rated between 90% and 99% are known as Premier Crus; and then you go down the ladder to the Deuxième Crus villages that are rated 80% – 89%.

By the CIVC`s regulations all champagne grapes must be hand harvested. The Comité tells growers when to pick and when to stop, usually a three-week window. The final yield must be no more than 66 hectoliters her hectare.

They also mandate the amount of juice that can be pressed: around 4,000 kilograms of grapes can yield to between 2,550 and 3,060 liters of juice. The first juice that comes from the press is the *cuvée* and the next 500 to 600 liters is the *taille* which is fermented separately.
The wines are blended to the producer`s house style and then given a secondary fermentation in the bottle that you will purchase. A small amount of yeast and 18 grams of sugar in liquid form (called *liqueur de tirage*) are added to each bottle which is then stoppered with a crown cap. The yeast eats the sugar, converting it to carbon dioxide gas and alcohol. The gas dissolves into the wine as bubbles; but there is a bi-product that has to be cleaned out – the sticky, dead yeast cells that accumulate on the side of the bottle.

The traditional way to clean out the sediment was by putting the bottles into an A-frame and a *remueur* would agitate the bottles by hand over a period of weeks, gradually tilting them upwards until all the debris has settled on the crown cap. (This process has been mechanised by the use of gyro palettes which allows 504 bottles in a metal cage to be agitated.) The inverted bottles would then be dipped into a glycol solution to freeze an inch or so of wine in the neck. The bottle would be opened and the pressure of the gas (90lbs per square inch, bus type pressure) would drive out a plug of ice containing the debris leaving the wine crystal-clear.

With the loss of a couple of ounces of wine the bottles have to be topped up and it`s at this point that the producer decides on the house style of the champagne by adding a *liqueur d'expédition,* a mixture of wine and sugar. The amount of sugar determines the sweetness level of the champagne. (Some producers cut the sugar to a minimum to produce the driest champagnes they designate as Brut Nature or Zero Dosage.)

And then there are the bubbles.

Someone in Champagne has established that there are 150 – 200 million bubbles in a 750mL bottle. Thirty to 35 bubbles are created per second and they rise at a speed of 35 kilometres an hour. When a bubble bursts it forms the shape of a flower with petals. The pressure ejects a champagne cork at a speed of 65 kph for the first 10 feet. (Whoever made these observations must have too much time on his hands.)

LAS VEGAS HERE WE COME…AND GO

Friday, March 13th: Up at 4:30 am to walk Rosie the Rescue before leaving for the airport at 5:30 for our trip to Las Vegas. An excellent Air Canada Rouge flight (half empty). As soon as you step off the plane into the airport you are greeted by banks of slot machines.

Taxied to the Mandalay Bay Hotel, where our room was not ready, so we went to lunch at The Blues Room. On the wall, framed behind glass, was a guitar, owned by Santana, with an embroidered body. Deborah ordered Voodoo Shrimp and I, a BBQ brisket nacho disc. Both were listed under appetizers although they were a full meal in themselves. The wine: Ferrari-Carano Chardonnay 2017.

After lunch we returned to the front desk to find we had been upgraded to a magnificent suite on the 62nd floor overlooking the pool complex.

A two-hour nap and then left the hotel to the Zappos Theatre at Planet Hollywood. We had booked tickets for Shania Twain's "Let's Go" concert, the opening night. Not the easiest journey, which involved taking two tram cars that were not simple to access. To reach the theatre we had to walk through the casino. That seems to be the architectural imperative here – to get anywhere you have to walk through walls of slot machines and card desks in Planet Hollywood.

The show started 40 minutes late. Apparently, Shania had injured her right foot playing football with her dog and couldn't move freely around the stage. But it was a great show; the production with back projections was fabulous, as were the male dancers. Shania was in great form and the sold-out audience loved her. Took a taxi back to the hotel.

Saturday, March 14th: Hearing from friends back in Canada that anyone who has left Canada and is returning from another county should go into to self-isolation for two weeks!!

Had breakfast in the Penthouse Lounge on our floor. Since we're in Vegas, decided to gamble. Played the 1 cent slot machines (big gambler). Won $26.45 US (which is about $500 Canadian). Cashed out – not a bad investment for $2.

Then took the tram to the Luxor-Excalibur stop to walk the strip. We were approached by two women in S&M gear toting handcuffs and crops. One of them said to Deborah, "Is he bothering you? We could give him the treatment."

Deborah declined. (Later on, the walk we saw them administering punishment to some poor sad sack while his girlfriend? wife? filmed him being administered to.

Dropped in at Illy for a coffee before proceeding to the Bellagio for lunch at Noodles (deep-fried octopus and very spicy noodle soup, Deborah's with shrimp, mine with duck).

Dropped into the Bellagio to see the extraordinary Chihuly glass sculpture ceiling in the reception area, and the Chinese Year of the Rat installation in the hotel's atrium.
Then off by bus to find the Total Wine store in Town Square. First dropped into Whole Foods, where I purchased bottles of Whitehaven Sauvignon Blanc 2019 ($17.99 US), Sonoma-Cutrer Chardonnay Sonoma Coast $2018 ($19.99) and Jadot Combe aux Jacques Beaujolais-Villages 2015 ($19.99).

Total had a magnificent collection of single malts but not the one I was hoping to find: Edradour in Pitlochry, which used to be the smallest distillery in Scotland – a title now claimed by Strathearn, also in Perthshire.

To improve my mood, I picked up a bottle of Le Haut-Médoc de Haut-Bages Libéral 2015 ($29.95 US).

Bussed back to the Mandalay Bay and sat down to a glass of the Whitehaven Sauvignon. Note to self: do not try to drink Sauvignon Blanc immediately after crunching up a Pepto-Bismol tablet. (Trying to settle my stomach in anticipation of tonight's dinner at Picasso in the Bellagio hotel. Should have relied on the Sauvignon Blanc.)

Picasso has the best list of Spanish wines in North America and a truly memorable tasting menu. We began with an amuse-bouche of butternut squash soup in an egg-cup-sized dish with a pheasant croquette on the side. Then came the tasting menu. (To ensure you do not salivate all over the age, I will not go into detail about the parade of dishes.)

But here are the accompanying wines: half bottle of Domaine Weinbach Riesling Schlossberg 2016, followed by a bottle of Torres Mas La Plana Gran Coronas 1994. My dessert was a pistachio lime soufflé with raspberry sorbet. Deborah's was a lemon concoction, but I was too busy enjoying mine to record what she ate.

Sunday, March 15th: Receiving emails from home telling us to come back immediately, otherwise we might get stuck in Las Vegas. Sounds like warnings out of Dante's Inferno. Contacted our wonderful travel agent, Sandra Pauwels of Pauwels Travel, who immediately got in touch with Air Canada to try and get us on the red-eye flight tonight.

To assuage our troubled souls, Deborah went dress shopping and I to donate cash to the slot machines across from the store from which she emerged with four dresses (Deborah corrected me saying they weren't dresses, they were tops. They looked like dresses to me).

Then we went out for lunch at Eataly (where we lunched on great pizza slices) before wandering around The Shops at Crystals (a magnificent building designed by Daniel Libeskind, who did the addition to the ROM). Dropped into a store that sold William Carr photography and was tempted to buy a shot of a waterfall that looked like a torrent of flames (see his work at www.artbrokerage.com/William-Carr).

Walked back to the hotel through a haze of weed smoke (the Las Vegas air is rancid with the smell of marijuana). Got the welcome news that our travel agent was able to book us on the 12:50 pm flight tomorrow to Toronto. So, we have one last dinner in Vegas: at Guy Savoy in Caesar's Palace.

And what a meal! As the *amuse-bouches* arrived so did a trolley of breads, a mountain of butter and the best olive oil I've tasted. Then a chopped oyster with chives, lemon oi and oyster juice set on a bed of seaweed. Deborah ordered the chef's specialty, artichoke and black truffle soup, followed by wagyu beef; and I the chicken, foie gras and artichoke terrine, followed by roasted quail. The wines, half bottles of Pascal Jolivet Sancerre 2016 and Flaiveley Mercurey 2003.

No room for dessert so we ordered digestifs – Green Chartreuse and Trimbach Grande Réserve Poire William. But along came a trolley and we couldn't resist a small pot of crème caramel and a tiny slice of cheesecake. To cleanse the palate, Earl Grey sorbet with black pepper. A truly memorable gastronomic affair.

Monday, March 16th: Awoke to see a flashing red light on the phone: a message from the management that everyone had to check out of the hotel by noon. All MGM properties were closing down. Took the shuttle to the airport and boarded our Air Canada flight to Toronto.

ABOUT THE AUTHOR

Tony Aspler is an internationally known writer, speaker, and wine expert, based in St. Catharines, Ontario. He has been writing about wine for over 50 years. He was the wine columnist for The Toronto Star for 21 years and has authored nineteen books on wine and food, including *The Wine Atlas of Canada*, *Vintage Canada*, *The Wine Lover's Companion*, *The Wine Lover Cooks*, *Travels with My Corkscrew* and *Tony Aspler's Cellar Book*.

He is the author/co-author of nine novels, including three with Gordon Pape: *Chain Reaction*, *The Scorpion Sanction*, and *The Music Wars*.

His latest series is a collection of wine murder mysteries featuring the itinerant wine writer/detective Ezra Brant: *Blood Is Thicker than Beaujolais*, *The Beast of Barbaresco* and *Death on the Douro*. He is currently working on *Nightmare in Napa*.

In December 2007, Tony was awarded the Order of Canada.

In 2012 Tony was the first Canadian to be inducted into the New York Media Wine Writers Hall of Fame. He was awarded the Queen's Jubilee Medal.

In 2017 Tony was awarded Spain's Officers Cross of the Order of Civil Merit.

In February 2001, Tony co-founded a charitable foundation in Toronto with Arlene Willis, called Grapes for Humanity (www.grapesforhumanity.com).

Tony Aspler's website can be found
at www.tonyaspler.com.

Made in the USA
Monee, IL
23 April 2021

66610799R00080